Elementary Art: 100 Years of Sherlock Holmes

First Published in 2017 by
Silver Screen Collectibles
PO Box 523
Hawthorne, CA 90251
www.SilverScreenCollectibles.com

Library of Congress Cataloging-in-Publication Data

Major, William S.
Elementary Art: 100 Years of Sherlock Holmes
edited by William S. Major.

ISBN: 978-0-9988239-0-4

Acknowledgements

This book would not have been possible without the generosity of Sherlock Holmes collector extrodinare, Ronald "Ronnie" James, and his unpresidented collection of Holmes posters and images.

Special Thanks to:
Denise Major
Bob Kotsopoulos
Jim Pauley
Gina Leslie
Jack Ong

This book is dedicated to the two most important girls in my life;
my wife Denise, and our daughter Cassidy.
Their boundless love and encouragement
inspired me to complete this project.

To Mike
All the best

CONTENTS

Introduction

Is Conan Doyle Right? is the name of a relatively obscure short film from 1923 out of Pathe Studios that explores the subject of spiritualism and the afterlife, a subject of great interest to Sir Arthur Conan Doyle.

Doyle's interest in spiritualism is said to have been cultivated by the grief he felt over the loss of his father and potentially his desire to *speak* with him again. Whether or not Conan Doyle was right is a matter of speculation and imagination, but it is no speculation that more than 80 years after his own death, his greatest creation continues to speak to fans around the world. On the next few pages, you will find extremely rare movie art from this unusual film.

From four novels (*A Study in Scarlet*, *The Sign of the Four*, *The Hound of the Baskervilles* and *The Valley of Fear*) as well as 56 short stories, Sir Arthur Conan Doyle has given the world over 125 years of Sherlockian adventures.

Starting from his 1887 creation, Holmes' character traits have woven themselves into the fabric of our society. It is hard to think of any detective story or mystery without The Great Detective popping into our minds.

In the pages to follow, you will see hundreds of Holmes stage and film posters, many of which have not been seen by the public since they were originally displayed, in some cases, more than 100 years ago. Several of the items that have been photographed for this book are the only copies known to exist.

Along with unfolding the progressive development of Holmes' character through the years, you will also see its effect on popular culture. The demonstration of this effect will be shown through poster images of many of the films which were inspired by Sir Arthur Conan Doyle's greatest literary creation.

I hope you enjoy the stunning images of over 100 years of the incomparable Sherlock Holmes.

A sketch of Sir Arthur Conan Doyle, from the files of the Los Angeles Herald Examiner.

Above: Lady (Jean) Doyle, Sir Arthur Conan Doyle, Mary Pickford, and Douglas Fairbanks.

Taken in Los Angeles, CA at the Pickford / Fairbanks Studio, May 25th, 1923. Ms. Pickford was filming "Rosita" at the time this photo was taken.

Sir ARTHUR CONAN DOYLE (*seated*) and WATTERSON R. ROTHACKER

Producer Watterson Rothacker (standing) with Sir Arthur Conan Doyle, who made his screen debut in "The Lost World" (1925).

Is Conan Doyle Right? (September 1923)
US 27 x 41 in (69 x 104 cm)

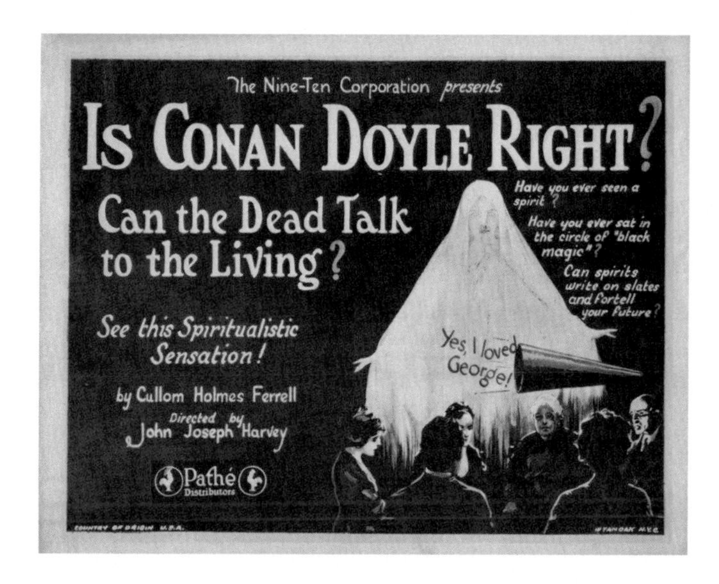

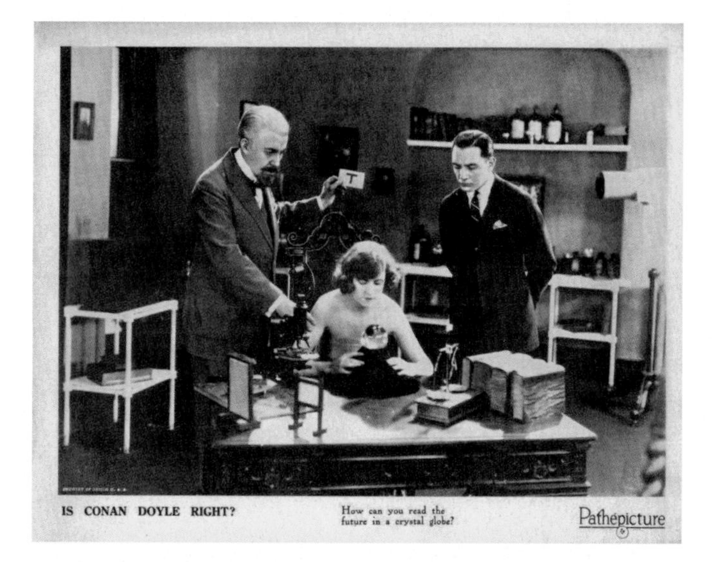

Is Conan Doyle Right? (September 1923)
US 11 x 14 in (28 x 36 cm)

Prologue

It is impossible to take you through the films of Sherlock Holmes without recognizing William Gillette. A dozen or so years after Sir Arthur Conan Doyle penned *A Study in Scarlet*, Holmes hit the stage for the first time. The Sherlock Holmes that most of the world has come to know is actually American actor/writer William Gillette's interpretation of Holmes. Gillette, working with Conan Doyle, wrote a stage play (with himself in the title role) based on Doyle's book. Gillette was also responsible for developing many of Holmes' signature traits, including the signature curved pipe, magnifying glass, the violin and even one of the most well-known phrases in the English language: "It's elementary, my dear Watson".

Below: Photos taken during Gillette's November 6, 1899 – June 16, 1900 run at the Garrick theatre in New York City, NY.

L-R: Thomas McGrath (Count von Stalburg), Harold Heaton (Sir Edward Leighton), William Gillette (Sherlock Holmes), Katherine Florence (Alice Faulkner), Bruce McRae (Dr. John Watson), Hilda England (Therese).

L-R: Judith Berolde (Madge Larrabee), Ralph Demore (James Larrabee), William Gillette (Sherlock Holmes), Ruben Fax (Benjamin Forman).

L-R: Ralph Demore (James Larrabee), William Gillette (Sherlock Holmes), Ruben Fax (Benjamin Forman).

L-R: Soldene Powell (Parsons), Henry McArdle (Billy the page boy), William Gillette (Sherlock Holmes), Bruce McRae (Dr. John Watson), Ruben Fax (Benjamin Forman disguised as a cabman), Judith Berolde (Madge Larrabee).

GARRICK THEATRE

HOYT & McKEE,
Lessees,
Also Lessees Madison Square Theatre.

CHARLES FROHMAN, Manager,
Also Manager of the Empire, Criterion, Garden and Madison Square Theatres, New York City, and the DUKE OF YORK'S THEATRE, LONDON, ENG.

Evenings, 8.15. Matinee Saturday, at 2.15.

MR. CHARLES FROHMAN PRESENTS
FOR THE FIRST TIME
A DRAMA IN FOUR ACTS
BY WILLIAM GILLETTE
AND A. CONAN DOYLE
ENTITLED

SHERLOCK HOLMES

BEING A HITHERTO UNPUBLISHED EPISODE
IN THE CAREER OF THE GREAT DETECTIVE
AND SHOWING HIS CONNECTION WITH THE
STRANGE CASE OF MISS FAULKNER

CHARACTERS IN THE PLAY	COMPANY APPEARING IN THE CAST
SHERLOCK HOLMES	WILLIAM GILLETTE
DOCTOR WATSON	BRUCE McRAE
JOHN FORMAN	RUBEN FAX
SIR EDWARD LEIGHTON	HAROLD HEATON
COUNT VON STAHLBURG	ALFRED S. HOWARD
PROFESSOR MORIARTY	GEORGE WESSELLS
JAMES LARRABEE	RALPH DELMORE
SIDNEY PRINCE	GEORGE HONEY
ALFRED BASSICK	HENRY HERRMAN
JIM CRAIGIN	THOMAS McGRATH
THOMAS LEARY	ELWYN EATON
"LIGHTFOOT" MCTAGUE	JULIUS WEYMS
JOHN	HENRY S. CHANDLER
PARSONS	SOLDENE POWELL
BILLY	HENRY McARDLE
ALICE FAULKNER	KATHERINE FLORENCE
MRS. FAULKNER	JANE THOMAS
MADGE LARRABEE	JUDITH BEROLDE
THÉRÈSE	HILDA ENGLUND
MRS. SMEEDLEY	EDITH TOTTEN

THE PLACE IS LONDON
THE TIME EIGHT YEARS AGO

FIRST ACT—DRAWING ROOM AT THE LARRABEES'—EVENING

SECOND ACT—SCENE I—PROFESSOR MORIARTY'S UNDERGROUND OFFICE—MORNING

SCENE II—SHERLOCK HOLMES' ROOMS IN BAKER STREET—EVENING

THIRD ACT—THE STEPNEY GAS CHAMBER—MIDNIGHT

FOURTH ACT—DOCTOR WATSON'S OFFICE—KENSINGTON—THE FOLLOWING EVENING

Garrick Theatre Program
Sherlock Holmes "Strange Case of Miss Faulkner"

"Sherlock Holmes" Original Royal Lyceum Theatre, London

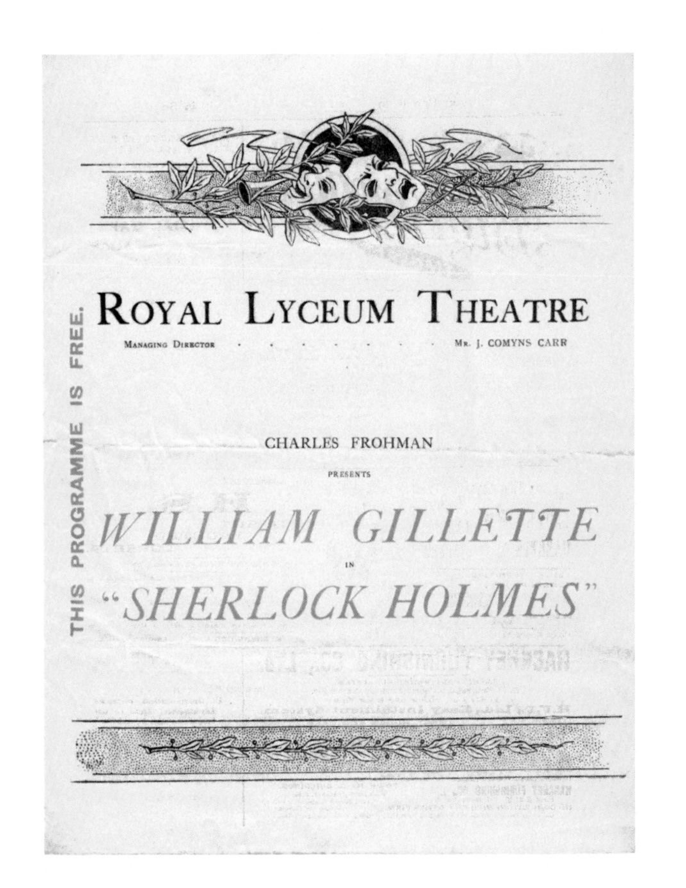

THIS PROGRAMME IS FREE.

ROYAL LYCEUM THEATRE

MANAGING DIRECTOR - - - - - - - - MR. J. COMYNS CARR

CHARLES FROHMAN

PRESENTS

WILLIAM GILLETTE

IN

"SHERLOCK HOLMES"

If you See it in "THE SUN" it is So.

His Majesty The King. Her Majesty The Queen.

Brinsmead

PIANOS

JOHN BRINSMEAD & SONS, LTD. 18, 20 & 22, Wigmore Street, London, W.

WHOSE ACTING DO YOU PREFER in this Play? If you send a post-card voting WITH THE MAJORITY to the Proprietors of WRIGHT'S COAL TAR SOAP, (Used throughout this Theatre.) SOUTHWARK, LONDON. They will send you a Tablet FREE.

All Communications respecting Advertisement Space on this Programme must be made to

C. POOL & CO.,

90–3, FLEET STREET, E.C.
Telephone—847 Holborn

THE LADY'S GAZETTE. Thursdays, 2d. NEW LADIES' PAPER.

FULLY ILLUSTRATED. SOMETHING NEW. SMART, CONCISE, INTERESTING.

A 6d. Paper for 2d.

CLOCK HOUSE, ARUNDEL ST., STRAND.

The Celebrated H.S. STRAIGHT FRONTED CORSETS.

Awarded GOLD MEDAL Exhibition 1900.

A Perfect and Graceful Figure assured to every lady wearing the H.S. CORSETS

Of all DRAPERS and LADIES' OUTFITTERS.

Prices, 3/11, 5/11, 7/11, 10/6 to 21/- per pair.

Should any difficulty arise in procuring, send Postal Order, size of waist and colour required, to the Manufacturers,

H. SHERWOOD & CO., 12, London Wall, E.C.

HACKNEY FURNISHING CO., LTD.

GRAND PROFIT-SHARING SYSTEM.

No Middleman and consequently no Middle Profits to pay.

25 per cent. below any other Firm.

H.F.C., Ltd., Easy Instalment System.

BEST HOUSE FOR CASH.

10 per cent. Discount for Cash. Carriage Free up to 300 miles.

Carpets and Linoleums Laid Free.

Send for Illustrated Catalogue and Prospectus (Post Free).

Deposit Optional. No Interest. Free Life Insurance.

Terms *pro rata* quoted up to any amount.

HACKNEY FURNISHING CO., LTD., Hours 9 till 9. Thursdays close 4.

NO CONNECTION WITH ANY OTHER FIRM.

On leaving Hackney Station, ask for the New Town Hall.

TOWN HALL BUILDINGS, Mare Street, Hackney, N.E.; Telegrams—"Furniments, London." Telephone—84, Dalston. Our Extensive Premises adjoin.

All Communications respecting Advertisement Space on this Programme must be made to

C. POOL & CO.,

90–3, FLEET STREET, E.C.
Telephone—847 Holborn.

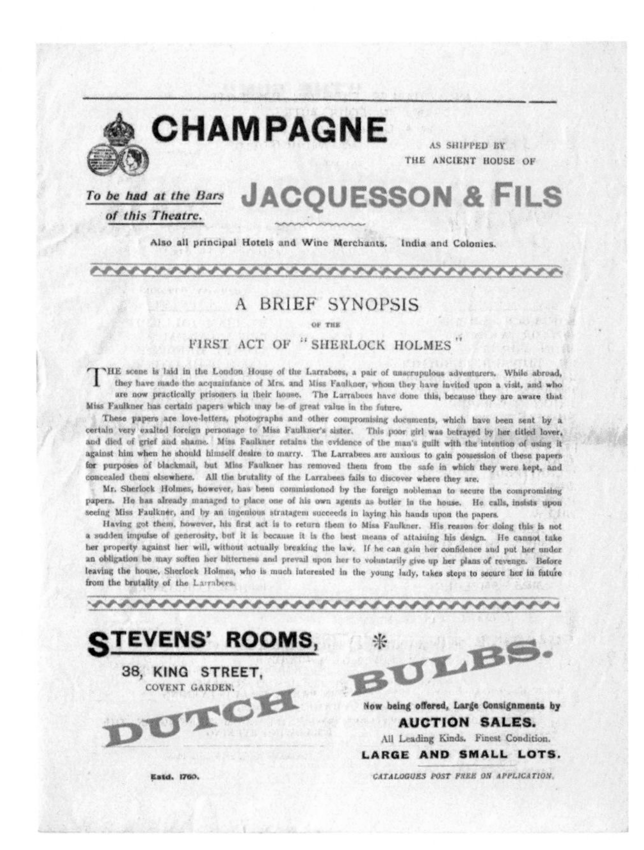

CHAMPAGNE

AS SHIPPED BY THE ANCIENT HOUSE OF

To be had at the Bars of this Theatre.

JACQUESSON & FILS

Also all principal Hotels and Wine Merchants. India and Colonies.

A BRIEF SYNOPSIS

OF THE

FIRST ACT OF "SHERLOCK HOLMES"

THE scene is laid in the London House of the Larrabees, a pair of unscrupulous adventurers. While abroad, they have made the acquaintance of Mrs. and Miss Faulkner, whom they have invited upon a visit, and who are now practically prisoners in their house. The Larrabees have done this, because they are aware that Miss Faulkner has certain papers which may be of great value in the future.

These papers are love-letters, photographs and other compromising documents, which have been sent by a certain very exalted foreign personage to Miss Faulkner's sister. This poor girl was betrayed by her titled lover, and died of grief and shame. Miss Faulkner retains the evidence of the man's guilt with the intention of using it against him when he should himself desire to marry. The Larrabees are anxious to gain possession of these papers for purposes of blackmail, but Miss Faulkner has removed them from the safe in which they were kept, and concealed them elsewhere. All the brutality of the Larrabees fails to discover where they are.

Mr. Sherlock Holmes, however, has been commissioned by the foreign nobleman to secure the compromising papers. He has already managed to place one of his own agents as butler in the house. He calls, insists upon seeing Miss Faulkner, and by an ingenious stratagem succeeds in laying his hands upon the papers.

Having got them, however, his first act is to return them to Miss Faulkner. His reason for doing this is not a sudden impulse of generosity, but it is because it is the best means of attaining his design. He cannot take her property against her will, without actually breaking the law. If he can gain her confidence and put her under an obligation he may soften her bitterness and prevail upon her to voluntarily give up her plans of revenge. Before leaving the house, Sherlock Holmes, who is much interested in the young lady, takes steps to secure her in future from the brutality of the Larrabees.

STEVENS' ROOMS,

38, KING STREET,
COVENT GARDEN.

DUTCH BULBS.

Now being offered, Large Consignments by AUCTION SALES.

All Leading Kinds. Finest Condition.

LARGE AND SMALL LOTS.

Estd. 1760.

CATALOGUES POST FREE ON APPLICATION.

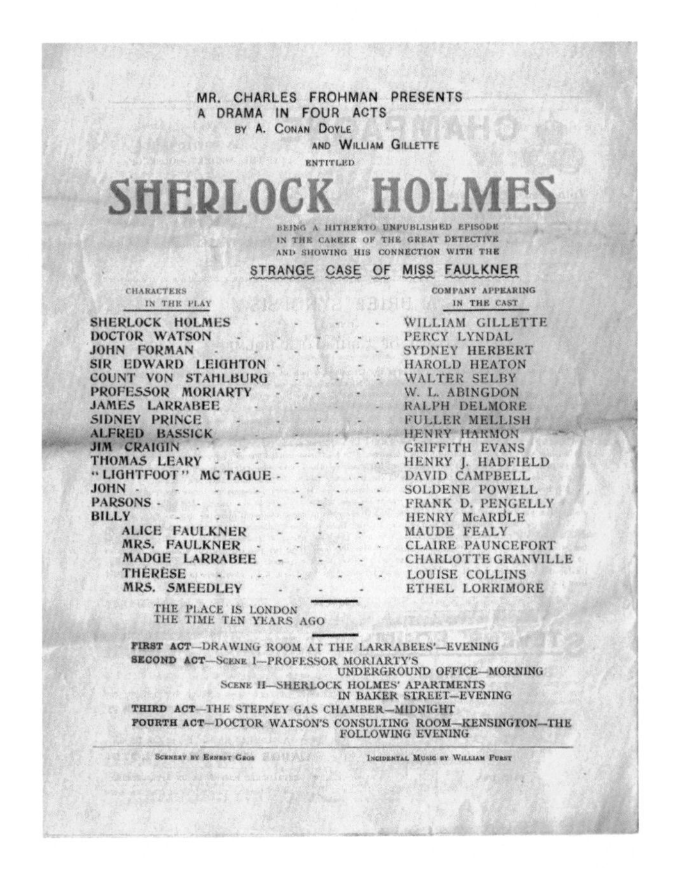

MR. CHARLES FROHMAN PRESENTS
A DRAMA IN FOUR ACTS
BY A. CONAN DOYLE
AND WILLIAM GILLETTE
ENTITLED

SHERLOCK HOLMES

BEING A HITHERTO UNPUBLISHED EPISODE
IN THE CAREER OF THE GREAT DETECTIVE
AND SHOWING HIS CONNECTION WITH THE

STRANGE CASE OF MISS FAULKNER

CHARACTERS IN THE PLAY	COMPANY APPEARING IN THE CAST
SHERLOCK HOLMES	WILLIAM GILLETTE
DOCTOR WATSON	PERCY LYNDAL
JOHN FORMAN	SYDNEY HERBERT
SIR EDWARD LEIGHTON	HAROLD HEATON
COUNT VON STAHLBURG	WALTER SELBY
PROFESSOR MORIARTY	W. L. ABINGDON
JAMES LARRABEE	RALPH DELMORE
SIDNEY PRINCE	FULLER MELLISH
ALFRED BASSICK	HENRY HARMON
JIM CRAIGIN	GRIFFITH EVANS
THOMAS LEARY	HENRY J. HADFIELD
"LIGHTFOOT" MC TAGUE	DAVID CAMPBELL
JOHN	SOLDENE POWELL
PARSONS	FRANK D. PENGELLY
BILLY	HENRY McARDLE
ALICE FAULKNER	MAUDE FEALY
MRS. FAULKNER	CLAIRE PAUNCEFORT
MADGE LARRABEE	CHARLOTTE GRANVILLE
THÉRÈSE	LOUISE COLLINS
MRS. SMEEDLEY	ETHEL LORRIMORE

THE PLACE IS LONDON
THE TIME TEN YEARS AGO

FIRST ACT—DRAWING ROOM AT THE LARRABEES'—EVENING
SECOND ACT—SCENE I—PROFESSOR MORIARTY'S UNDERGROUND OFFICE—MORNING
SCENE II—SHERLOCK HOLMES' APARTMENTS IN BAKER STREET—EVENING
THIRD ACT—THE STEPNEY GAS CHAMBER—MIDNIGHT
FOURTH ACT—DOCTOR WATSON'S CONSULTING ROOM—KENSINGTON—THE FOLLOWING EVENING

SCENERY BY ERNEST GROS — INCIDENTAL MUSIC BY WILLIAM FURST

Complete Program from December 1901 - April 1902 run

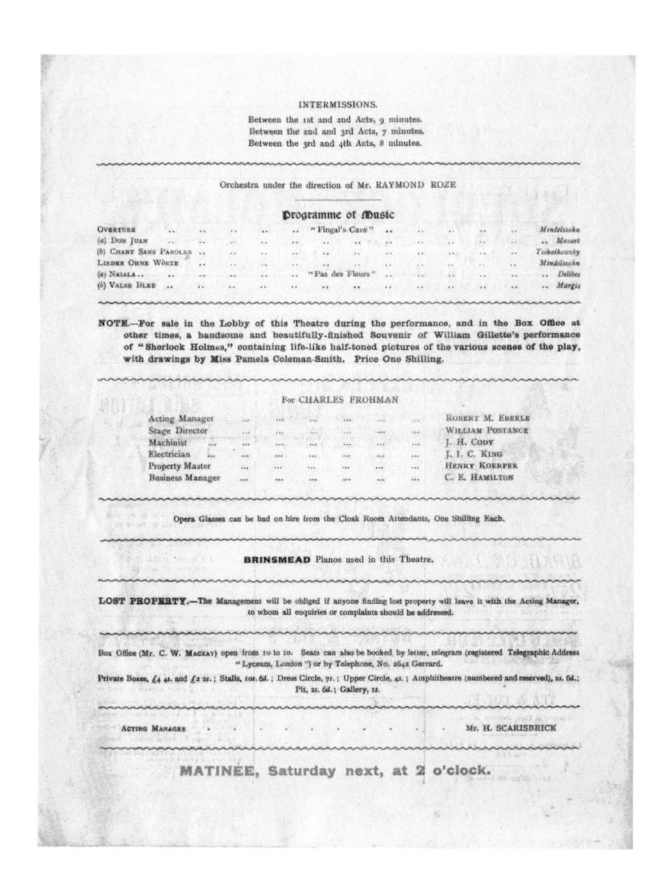

INTERMISSIONS.

Between the 1st and 2nd Acts, 9 minutes.
Between the 2nd and 3rd Acts, 7 minutes.
Between the 3rd and 4th Acts, 8 minutes.

Orchestra under the direction of Mr. RAYMOND ROZE

Programme of Music

Overture	"Fingal's Cave"	Mendelssohn
(a) Don Juan		Mozart
(b) Chant Sans Paroles		Tschaikowsky
Lieder Ohne Worte		Mendelssohn
(a) Naïla	"Pas des Fleurs"	Delibes
(b) Valse Bleu		Margis

NOTE.—For sale in the Lobby of this Theatre during the performance, and in the Box Office at other times, a handsome and beautifully-finished Souvenir of William Gillette's performance of "Sherlock Holmes," containing life-like half-toned pictures of the various scenes of the play, with drawings by Miss Pamela Coleman-Smith. Price One Shilling.

For CHARLES FROHMAN

Acting Manager	Robert M. Eberle
Stage Director	William Postance
Machinist	J. H. Cody
Electrician	J. I. C. King
Property Master	Henry Koerper
Business Manager	C. E. Hamilton

Opera Glasses can be had on hire from the Cloak Room Attendants, One Shilling Each.

BRINSMEAD Pianos used in this Theatre.

LOST PROPERTY.—The Management will be obliged if anyone finding lost property will leave it with the Acting Manager, to whom all enquiries or complaints should be addressed.

Box Office (Mr. C. W. Mackay) open from 10 to 10. Seats can also be booked by letter, telegram (registered Telegraphic Address "Lyceum, London") or by Telephone, No. 2642 Gerrard.

Private Boxes, £4 4s. and £2 2s.; Stalls, 10s. 6d.; Dress Circle, 7s.; Upper Circle, 4s.; Amphitheatre (numbered and reserved), 2s. 6d.; Pit, 2s. 6d.; Gallery, 1s.

Acting Manager . . . . Mr. H. SCARISBRICK

MATINEE, Saturday next, at 2 o'clock.

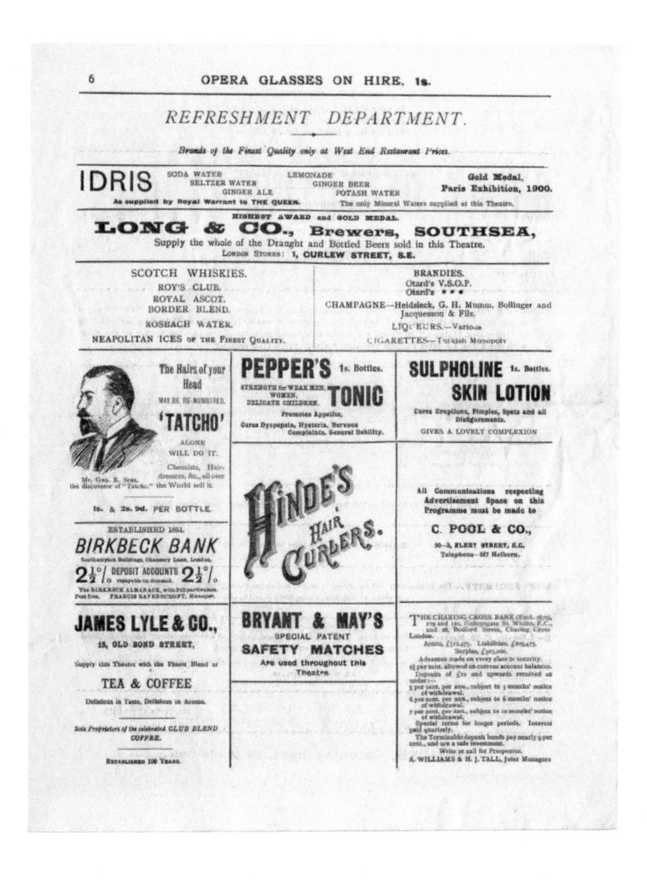

6 OPERA GLASSES ON HIRE, 1s.

REFRESHMENT DEPARTMENT.

Brands of the Finest Quality only at West End Restaurant Prices.

IDRIS SODA WATER, SELTZER WATER, GINGER ALE, LEMONADE, GINGER BEER, POTASH WATER. **Gold Medal, Paris Exhibition, 1900.**
As supplied by Royal Warrant to THE QUEEN. The only Mineral Waters supplied at this Theatre.

HIGHEST AWARD and GOLD MEDAL.
LONG & CO., Brewers, SOUTHSEA,
Supply the whole of the Draught and Bottled Beers sold in this Theatre.
London Stores: 1, CURLEW STREET, S.E.

SCOTCH WHISKIES. ROY'S CLUB. ROYAL ASCOT. BORDER BLEND. ROSBACH WATER. NEAPOLITAN ICES of the Finest Quality.

BRANDIES. Otard's V.S.O.P. Otard's * * * CHAMPAGNE—Heidsieck, G. H. Mumm, Bollinger and Jacquesson & Fils. LIQUEURS.—Various. CIGARETTES—Turkish Monopoly.

The Hairs of your Head MAY BE RE-NUMBERED. 'TATCHO' ALONE WILL DO IT. Chemists, Hairdressers, &c., all over the World sell it.
Mr. Geo. R. Sims, the discoverer of "Tatcho."
1s. & 2s. 9d. PER BOTTLE.

PEPPER'S TONIC 1s. Bottles. STRENGTH for WEAK MEN, WOMEN, DELICATE CHILDREN. Promotes Appetite, Cures Dyspepsia, Hysteria, Nervous Complaints, General Debility.

SULPHOLINE SKIN LOTION 1s. Bottles. Cures Eruptions, Pimples, Spots and all Disfigurements. GIVES A LOVELY COMPLEXION.

HINDE'S HAIR CURLERS.

ESTABLISHED 1851. **BIRKBECK BANK** Southampton Buildings, Chancery Lane, London. 2½% DEPOSIT ACCOUNTS 2½%. The BIRKBECK ALMANACK, with full particulars, Post free. FRANCIS RAVENSCROFT, Manager.

All Communications respecting Advertisement Space on this Programme must be made to C. POOL & CO., 90—3, FLEET STREET, E.C. Telephone—847 Holborn.

JAMES LYLE & CO., 15, OLD BOND STREET, Supply this Theatre with the Finest Blend of TEA & COFFEE. Delicious in Taste, Delicious in Aroma. Sole Proprietors of the celebrated CLUB BLEND COFFEE. Established 100 Years.

BRYANT & MAY'S SPECIAL PATENT **SAFETY MATCHES** Are used throughout this Theatre.

THE CHARING CROSS BANK (Estd. 1870), 119 and 120, Bishopsgate St. Within, E.C., and 28, Bedford Street, Charing Cross London.
Assets, £512,475. Liabilities, £209,475. Surplus, £303,000.
Advances made on every class of security.
2½ per cent. allowed on current account balances.
Deposits of £10 and upwards received as under:—
5 per cent. per ann., subject to 3 months' notice of withdrawal.
6 per cent. per ann., subject to 6 months' notice of withdrawal.
7 per cent. per ann., subject to 12 months' notice of withdrawal.
Special terms for longer periods. Interest paid quarterly.
The Terminable deposit bonds pay nearly 9 per cent., and are a safe investment.
Write or call for Prospectus.
A. WILLIAMS & H. J. TALL, Joint Managers

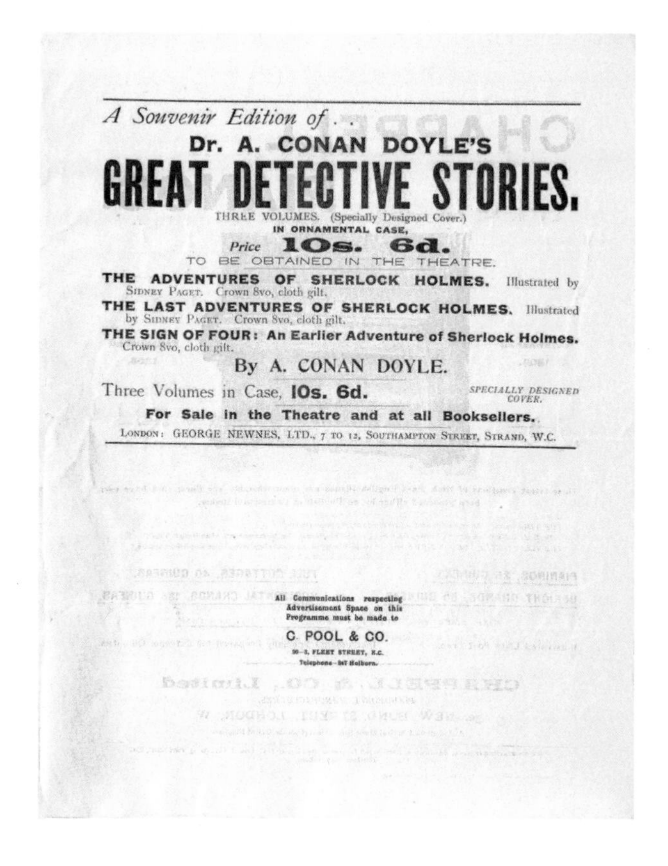

A Souvenir Edition of . .

Dr. A. CONAN DOYLE'S

GREAT DETECTIVE STORIES.

THREE VOLUMES. (Specially Designed Cover.)
IN ORNAMENTAL CASE,
Price **10s. 6d.**
TO BE OBTAINED IN THE THEATRE.

THE ADVENTURES OF SHERLOCK HOLMES. Illustrated by Sidney Paget. Crown 8vo, cloth gilt.

THE LAST ADVENTURES OF SHERLOCK HOLMES. Illustrated by Sidney Paget. Crown 8vo, cloth gilt.

THE SIGN OF FOUR: An Earlier Adventure of Sherlock Holmes. Crown 8vo, cloth gilt.

By A. CONAN DOYLE.

Three Volumes in Case, **10s. 6d.** *SPECIALLY DESIGNED COVER.*

For Sale in the Theatre and at all Booksellers.

London: GEORGE NEWNES, LTD., 7 to 12, Southampton Street, Strand, W.C.

All Communications respecting Advertisement Space on this Programme must be made to
C. POOL & CO.
90—3, FLEET STREET, E.C.
Telephone—847 Holborn.

CHAPPELL PIANOS.

Established 1808. Established 1808.

Their latest creations of High-class English Pianos are unquestionably the finest that have ever been produced either by an English or Continental maker.

THE TIMES says:—"A real Piano with a tone of remarkably sweet quality."
THE DAILY NEWS says:—"Combines the tone and power of a Grand with the compactness of an Upright Piano."
THE ILLUSTRATED LONDON NEWS says:—"Great delicacy of touch and abundance of tone-sustaining capacity."

PIANINOS, 25 GUINEAS. **FULL COTTAGES, 40 GUINEAS.**
UPRIGHT GRANDS, 50 GUINEAS. **HORIZONTAL CRANDS, 135 GUINEAS.**

HIRE, INSTALMENT SYSTEM, OR LIBERAL DISCOUNT FOR CASH.

Illustrated Lists Post Free. Instruments Specially Prepared for Extreme Climates.

CHAPPELL & CO., Limited,
PIANOFORTE MANUFACTURERS,
50, NEW BOND STREET, LONDON, W.
And of all the Principal Music Sellers throughout the United Kingdom.

All Communications respecting Advertisement Space on this Programme must be made to C. Pool & Co., *90—3, Fleet Street, E.C. Telephone—847 Holborn.*

William Gillette made a single appearance on film as Sherlock Holmes, in a 1916 silent version for the Essanay Film Manufacturing Company. This 100-year old film was long presumed lost, but, to the joy of Sherlock fans around the world, a nitrate duplicate negative was discovered in the film archives of the Cinémathèque Française in Paris, late in 2014.

Below are four original and extremely rare "mini" lobby cards from Gillette's 1916 feature, Sherlock Holmes.

Below: Two original photos of William Gillette, one of which is inscribed and signed by the actor.

Above: The inscription reads:
"Sincere Regards To Mrs. Hartley - William Gillette"

"It is too little to say William Gillette resembles Sherlock Holmes. Sherlock Holmes looks exactly like William Gillette."

- Orson Welles
Mercury Theater Broadcast
September 25th, 1938

FAREWELL TO THE STAGE

WILLIAM GILLETTE

in His Famous Creation

SHERLOCK HOLMES

by William Gillette & Sir Arthur Conan Doyle

DIRECTION of
A·L·ERLANGER &
GEORGE C·TYLER

Steele

FORD'S
THEATRE BALTIMORE

WEEK, BEGINNING
MON. JAN. 13
MATINEE SATURDAY ONLY

CAREY & SONS LITH N.Y.

PRINTED IN U.S.A.

Gillette performed numerous roles throughout his career, but Holmes had become his alter-ego. After more than 30 years of portraying Holmes, on November 15, 1929, William Gillette started his farewell tour.

Left: Original Farewell Tour poster for Gillette's Baltimore appearance, January 13th, 1930.

Right and Below: Farewell Tour photos, which may have been included in the souvenir booklet.

By the time William Gillette's Farewell Tour ended in Wilmington, DE, on March 19, 1932, it is believed that he gave approximately 1300 performances as Sherlock Holmes throughout his career.

To many Holmes fans, Gillette is second only to Doyle himself, in the importance of bringing Sherlock Holmes to life.

The Early Years

While William Gillette ruled the stage as Sherlock Holmes, for most people, the first "film Holmes" was Eille Norwood, who donned the deerstalker for 47 films between 1921 and 1923. Although Mr. Norwood's name was properly spelled "Eille", most US film advertising misspelled it as "Ellie"...just another Holmes mystery.

1920 Trade Ad, featuring Eille Norwood

The Beryl Coronet (February 1922)
UK 26½ x 40½ in (67 x 103 cm)

The following two pages:
The Hound of the Baskervilles (August 1921 - UK)
US 11 x 14 in (28 x 36 cm)

ELLIE NORWOOD
AS
SHERLOCK HOLMES
in
SIR ARTHUR CONAN DOYLE'S
GREATEST MYSTERY DRAMA
"THE HOUND OF
THE BASKERVILLES"
DISTRIBUTED BY FILM BOOKING OFFICES OF AMERICA
IT'S AN
R-C
PICTURE

"THE
HOUND OF THE
BASKERVILLES"
"I've seen it again - out
there on the moor"

But we must solve
this awful mystery-
"THE
HOUND OF THE
BASKERVILLES"

"Why did you signal from the
window at midnight?"
"THE
HOUND OF THE
BASKERVILLES"

The Sign of Four (June 1923 - UK)
Australia 15 x 40 in (38 x 102 cm)
"Australian Daybill"

Right: Sherlock Brown (June 1922)
US 11 x 14 in (28 x 36 cm)
Although not a direct spoof, this mystery-comedy featured a want-to-be detective (not) coincidentally named "Sherlock Brown"

BERT LYTELL
IN
SHERLOCK BROWN
METRO
PICTURES
REG. U. S. PAT. OFF.

BERT LYTELL
IN
SHERLOCK BROWN
METRO
PICTURES
REG. U. S. PAT. OFF.

Although Eille Norwood was well established in the U.K. as the Sherlock Holmes of his day, less than half of his films were released in the United States.

Hollywood, not wanting to miss out on the popularity of Holmes, engaged legendary stage and screen actor John Barrymore in 1922. Barrymore portrayed a very respectable Holmes, alongside Roland Young as Dr. Watson, Gustav von Seyffertitz as Professor Moriarty, William Powell as Foreman Wells, Reginald Denny as Prince Alexis, Hedda Hopper (future Hollywood gossip columnist) as Madge Larrabee, and Carol Dempster as non-Doyle love interest, Alice Faulkner.

The three lobby cards included from this film are all original release cards. The original pressbook gave theatres the option of purchasing either colorized or brown duo-tone versions of the cards.

Below and Right:
Sherlock Holmes (March 1922)
US 11 x 14 in (28 x 36 cm)

Fingerprints never lie!

Two master minds meet at the precipice of Death

Buster Keaton in Sherlock Jr. (1924)

May McAvoy & Edward Everett Horton in "The Terror" (1928)

German 'Herald' - Der Hund von Baskerville (1929)
with Carlyle Blackwell as Sherlock Holmes.

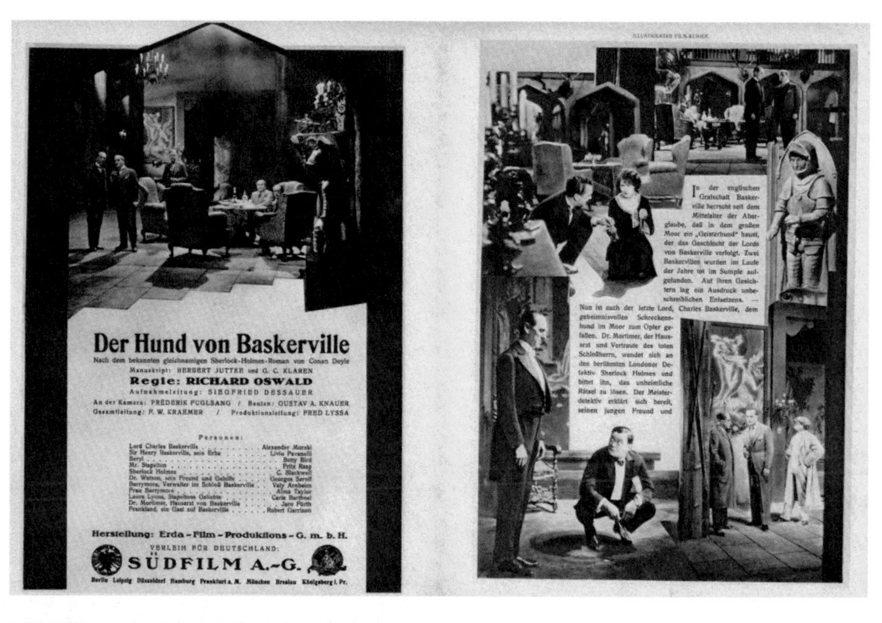

Der Hund von Baskerville

Nach dem bekannten gleichnamigen Sherlock-Holmes-Roman von Conan Doyle

Manuskript: HERBERT JUTTKE und G. C. KLAREN

Regie: RICHARD OSWALD

Aufnahmeleitung: SIEGFRIED DESSAUER

An der Kamera: FREDERIK FUGLSANG / Bauten: GUSTAV A. KNAUER

Gesamtleitung: F. W. KRAEMER / Produktionsleitung: FRED LYSSA

Personen:

Lord Charles Baskerville . . . . Alexander Murski
Sir Henry Baskerville, sein Erbe . . . . Livio Pavanelli
Beryl . . . . Betty Bird
Mr. Stapelton . . . . Fritz Rasp
Sherlock Holmes . . . . C. Blackwell
Dr. Watson, sein Freund und Gehilfe . . . . Georges Seroff
Barrymore, Verwalter im Schloß Baskerville . . . . Valy Arnheim
Frau Barrymore . . . . Alma Taylor
Laura Lyons, Stapeltons Geliebte . . . . Carla Bartheel
Dr. Mortimer, Hausarzt von Baskerville . . . . Jaro Fürth
Frankland, ein Gast auf Baskerville . . . . Robert Garrison

Herstellung: Erda-Film-Produktions-G. m. b. H.

VERLEIH FÜR DEUTSCHLAND:

SÜDFILM A.-G.

Berlin Leipzig Düsseldorf Hamburg Frankfurt a. M. München Breslau Königsberg i. Pr.

In der englischen Grafschaft Baskerville herrscht seit dem Mittelalter der Aberglaube, daß in dem großen Moor ein „Geisterhund" haust, der das Geschlecht der Lords von Baskerville verfolgt. Zwei Baskervilles wurden im Laufe der Jahre tot im Sumpfe aufgefunden. Auf ihren Gesichtern lag ein Ausdruck unbeschreiblichen Entsetzens. — Nun ist auch der letzte Lord, Charles Baskerville, dem geheimnisvollen Schreckenshund im Moor zum Opfer gefallen. Dr. Mortimer, der Hausarzt und Vertraute des toten Schloßherrn, wendet sich an den berühmten Londoner Detektiv Sherlock Holmes und bittet ihn, das unheimliche Rätsel zu lösen. Der Meisterdetektiv erklärt sich bereit, seinen jungen Freund und

Helfer, Dr. Watson, nach Baskerville zu schicken. — Gleichzeitig mit Dr. Watson kommt der neue Erbe von Baskerville, Sir Henry Baskerville, aus den Kolonien im Schlosse an. Dr. Watson macht sich sogleich mit Feuereifer an die Aufklärung des mysteriösen Falles. Im Schlosse und in dessen Umgebung findet er die folgenden Personen vor: Zunächst den seltsamen, verschlossenen und beinahe scheuen Hausverwalter Barrymore und dessen ängstlich herumschleichende, bleiche Frau. Dann den Gutsnachbarn von Baskerville, einen Mr. Stapelton, einen beinahe komischen Sonderling, der sein Hauptvergnügen darin findet, mit dem Schmetterlingsnetz und der Botanisiertrommel das Moor zu durchwandern. Ferner die Pflegetochter Stapeltons, Beryl, ein hübsches, junges Mädchen, das Dr. Watson unter besonders denkwürdigen Umständen kennenlernt.

Viele sonderbare und eigenartige Beobachtungen verwirren den jungen Doktor. Baskerville ist ein selten unheimlicher und rätselvoller Ort. Das alte Schloß scheint in der Nacht zu seltsamem Leben zu erwachen. Aus dem nahen, nachtschwarzen Moor ertönen Schreie und langgezogenes Heulen. Dr. Watson gewahrt in der Tat ein großes Tier mit glühenden Augen und feurigem Atem, das im Dunkel durch den Sumpf streift. Seine Spuren gleichen deutlich dem Abdruck riesiger Hundepfoten.

Einmal flieht ein Unbekannter mit fliegenden Rockschößen vor Dr. Watson in das undurchdringliche Dunkel des Moors. Der Doktor versucht vergeblich, den Flüchtigen einzuholen. Er versucht überhaupt vergeblich, Licht in diese dunkle Angelegenheit zu bringen. Und fühlt doch, wie sich die gefahrvolle Schlinge mehr und mehr um den Hals Sir Henrys legt, für dessen Leben er verantwortlich ist. Was ists mit dem grauenvollen „Hund von Baskerville"?

Während Dr. Watson von Rätsel zu Rätsel tappt, ist sein Freund und Meister Sherlock Holmes nicht müßig geblieben und dicht vor dem Ziel. Zwar fordert der Hund noch einmal ein Menschenleben zum Opfer. Aber es ist nicht der junge Erbe von Baskerville, trotzdem ihm der Anschlag gelten sollte. Dann bringt Sherlock Holmes den sagenhaften Hund zur Strecke und nach verzweifeltem, gefahrvollem Kampf auch den Teufel in Menschengestalt, der die Seele des historischen Verbrechens von Baskerville war.

Sound came to Sherlock for the first time in 1929 -- with Clive Brook in the lead role -- in *The Return of Sherlock Holmes.* Clive also starred in the 1932 Holmes feature, *Sherlock Holmes.* Along with his lead roles in these two Holmes features, he also donned his deerstalker for the 1930 feature *Paramount on Parade.*

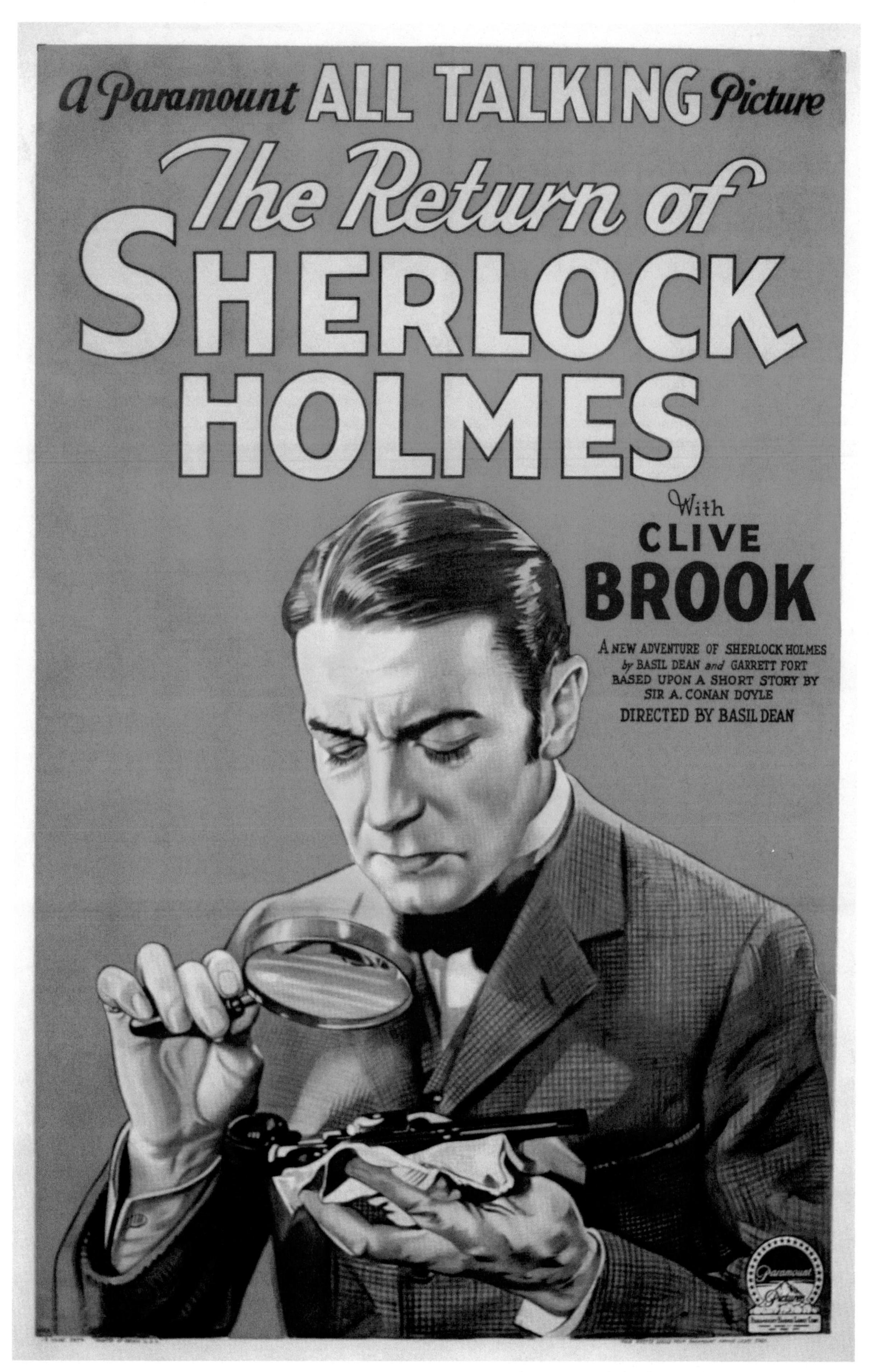

The Return of Sherlock Holmes (October 1929)
US 27 x 41 in (69 x 104 cm)

The following four pages:
The Return of Sherlock Holmes (October 1929)
US 11 x 14 in (28 x 36 cm)

The
RETURN of
SHERLOCK
HOLMES
WITH
CLIVE BROOK
A new adventure
of Sherlock Holmes
by Basil Dean and
Garrett Fort based up
on a short story by
Sir A. Conan Doyle.
DIRECTED BY
BASIL DEAN
A Paramount Picture
2914 COUNTRY OF ORIGIN U.S.A.
THIS LOBBY DISPLAY LEASED FROM PARAMOUNT FAMOUS

THE RETURN
of
SHERLOCK
HOLMES
WITH
CLIVE BROOK
A Paramount Picture
COUNTRY OF ORIGIN U. S. A.
THIS LOBBY DISPLAY LEASED FROM PARAMOUNT LASKY CORP

THE RETURN
of
SHERLOCK
HOLMES
CLIVE BROOK
COUNTRY OF ORIGIN U. S. A.
THIS LOBBY DISPLAY LEASED FROM PARAMOUNT LASKY CORP

THE RETURN
of
SHERLOCK
HOLMES
CLIVE BROOK
COUNTRY OF ORIGIN U. S. A.
THIS LOBBY DISPLAY LEASED FROM PARAMOUNT LASKY CORP

THE RETURN
of
SHERLOCK
HOLMES
CLIVE BROOK
COUNTRY OF ORIGIN U. S. A.
THIS LOBBY DISPLAY LEASED FROM PARAMOUNT LASKY CORP.

THE RETURN
of
SHERLOCK
HOLMES
CLIVE BROOK
COUNTRY OF ORIGIN U. S. A.
THIS LOBBY DISPLAY LEASED FROM PARAMOUNT LASKY CORP.

THE RETURN
of
SHERLOCK
HOLMES
CLIVE BROOK
COUNTRY OF ORIGIN U. S. A.
THIS LOBBY DISPLAY LEASED FROM PARAMOUNT LASKY CORP

THE RETURN
of
SHERLOCK
HOLMES
CLIVE BROOK
COUNTRY OF ORIGIN U. S. A.
THIS LOBBY DISPLAY LEASED FROM PARAMOUNT LASKY CORP

The Return of Sherlock Holmes (October 1929)
US 14 x 22 in (36 x 56 cm)

The Return of Sherlock Holmes (October 1929)
US 14 x 36 in (36 x 91 cm)

Sherlock Holmes (November 1932)
France 24½ x 33½ in (62 x 85 cm)

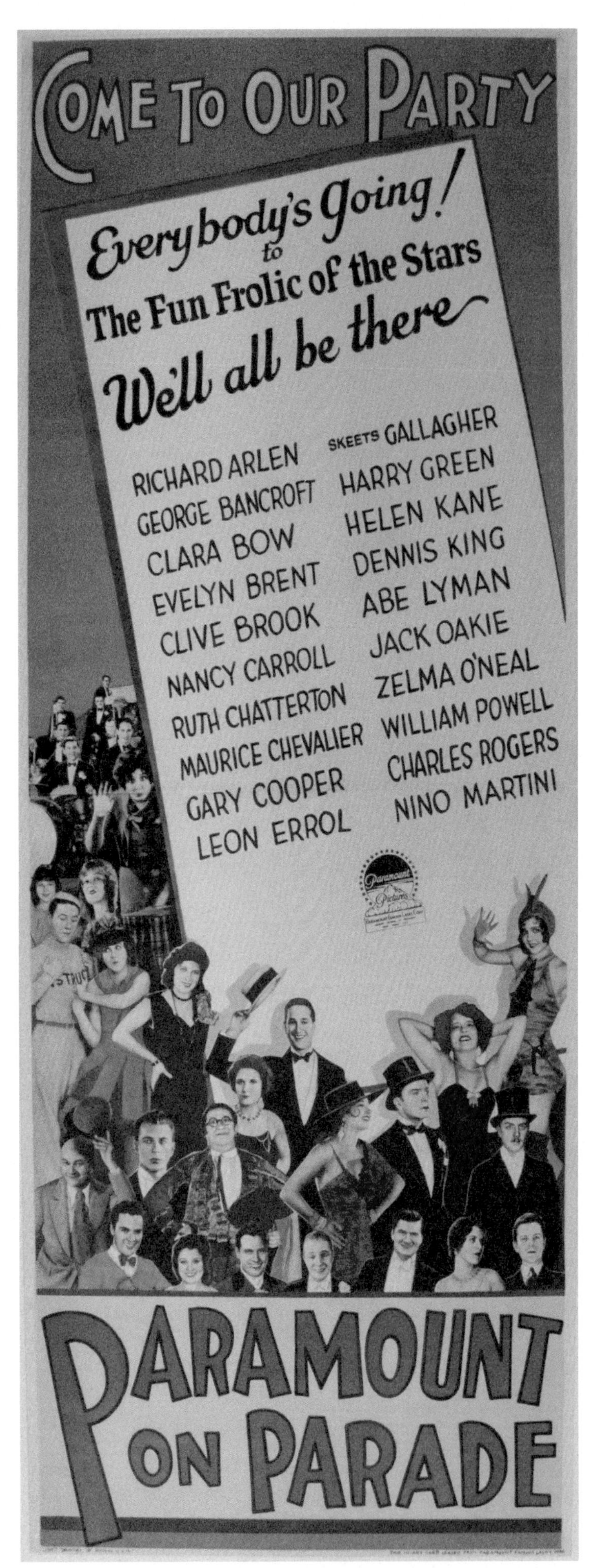

Paramount on Parade (April 1930)
US 14 x 36 in (36 x 91 cm)

William Powell and Clive Brook
Paramount on Parade publicity photo

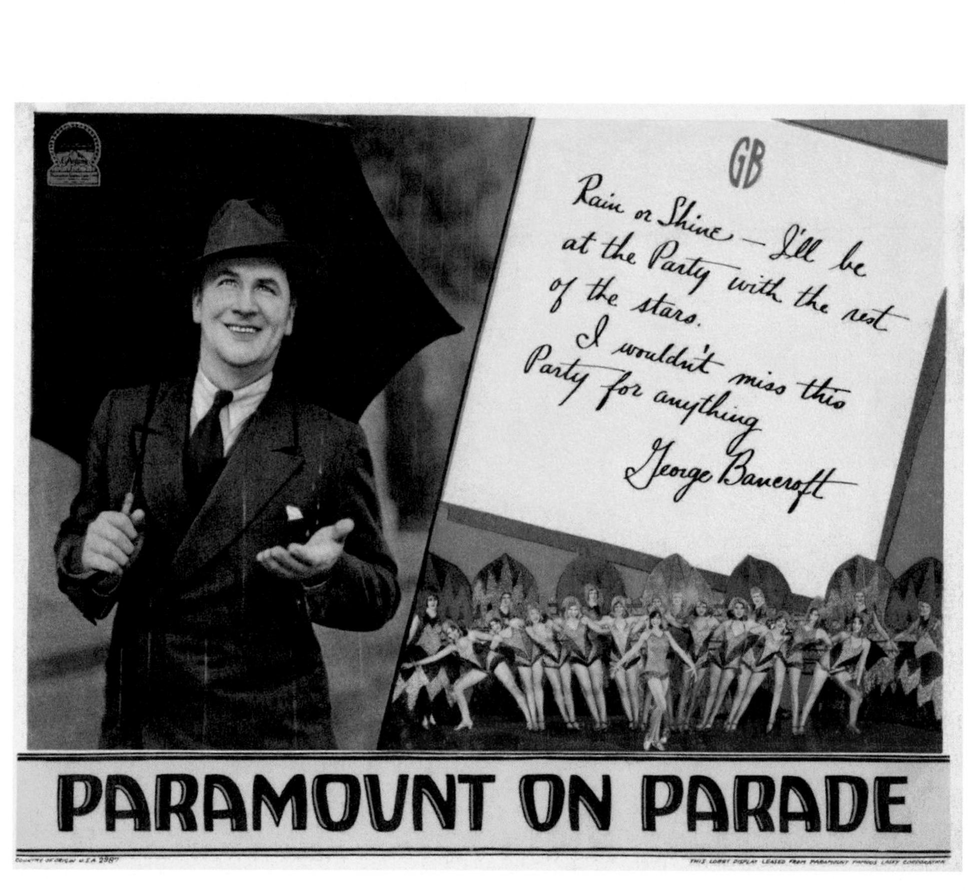

Paramount on Parade (April 1930)
US 11 x 14 in (28 x 36 cm)

Following Clive Brook's talkie debut, several studios capitalized on the popularity of Holmes with various actors making a single appearance in the lead role...none of whom seemed to capture the true essence of the character.

The Hound of the Baskervilles (1932) featured Robert Rendel in the lead role and Frederick Lloyd as Dr. Watson, in their only Holmes film. Panned by critics, potentially the best legacy of this film is the beautiful US "One-Sheet" poster, featured on the following page.

Raymond Massey took a turn in Conan Doyles' favorite Holmes story, *The Speckled Band* (1932).

Czechoslovakian actor/director/writer Martin Fric portrayed Holmes in two Czech films, *Lelícek ve sluzbách Sherlocka Holmese* (1932) and *Le roi bis* (1933).

The Hound of the Baskervilles (April 1932)
US 27 x 41 in (69 x 104 cm)

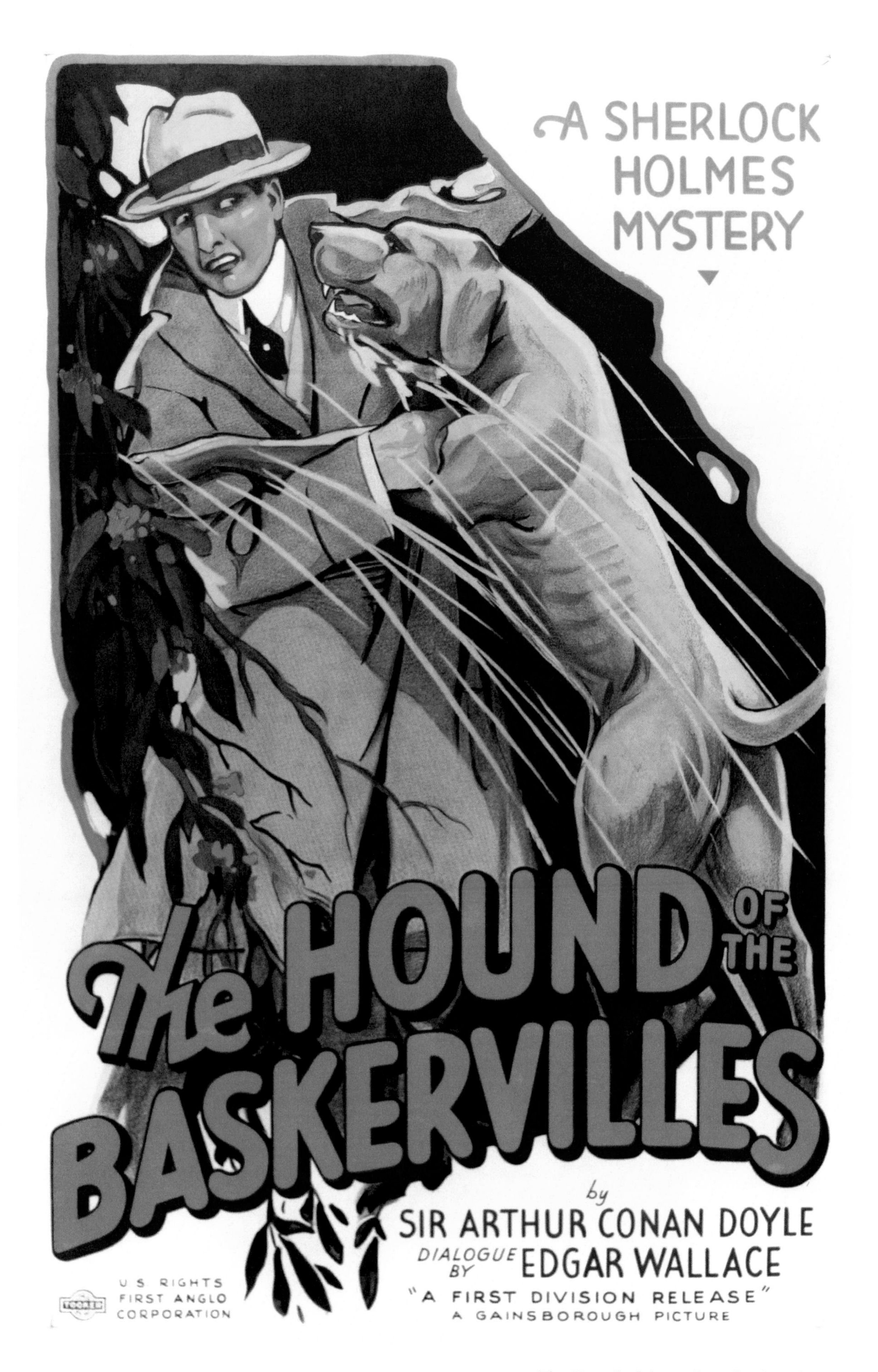

The Hound of the Baskervilles (April 1932)
US 27 x 41 in (69 x 104 cm)

On the heels of Clive Brook's foray into Sherlock, 56-year old Arthur Wontner started a five-film run as Sherlock Holmes with *Fatal Hour* (1931); *The Missing Rembrandt*, *The Sign of Four*, *The Triumph of Sherlock Holmes* and *Murder at the Baskervilles* round out his stint. Some critics and fans consider Wontner's portrayal of Holmes to be one of the best.

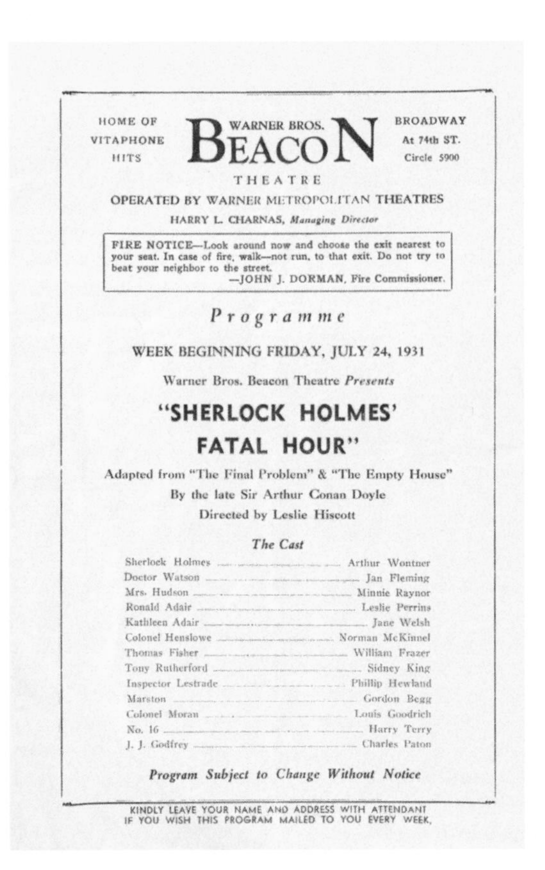

HOME OF VITAPHONE HITS

WARNER BROS. BEACON THEATRE

BROADWAY At 74th ST. Circle 5900

OPERATED BY WARNER METROPOLITAN THEATRES

HARRY L. CHARNAS, *Managing Director*

FIRE NOTICE—Look around now and choose the exit nearest to your seat. In case of fire, walk—not run, to that exit. Do not try to beat your neighbor to the street.
—JOHN J. DORMAN, Fire Commissioner.

Programme

WEEK BEGINNING FRIDAY, JULY 24, 1931

Warner Bros. Beacon Theatre *Presents*

"SHERLOCK HOLMES' FATAL HOUR"

Adapted from "The Final Problem" & "The Empty House"
By the late Sir Arthur Conan Doyle
Directed by Leslie Hiscott

The Cast

Sherlock Holmes	Arthur Wontner
Doctor Watson	Jan Fleming
Mrs. Hudson	Minnie Raynor
Ronald Adair	Leslie Perrins
Kathleen Adair	Jane Welsh
Colonel Henslowe	Norman McKinnel
Thomas Fisher	William Frazer
Tony Rutherford	Sidney King
Inspector Lestrade	Phillip Hewland
Marston	Gordon Begg
Colonel Moran	Louis Goodrich
No. 16	Harry Terry
J. J. Godfrey	Charles Paton

Program Subject to Change Without Notice

KINDLY LEAVE YOUR NAME AND ADDRESS WITH ATTENDANT IF YOU WISH THIS PROGRAM MAILED TO YOU EVERY WEEK.

Program Cover from the Warner Bros. Beacon Theatre (NYC) - July 24, 1931

England - “Triumph of Sherlock Holmes” pressbook
Released: February 1935

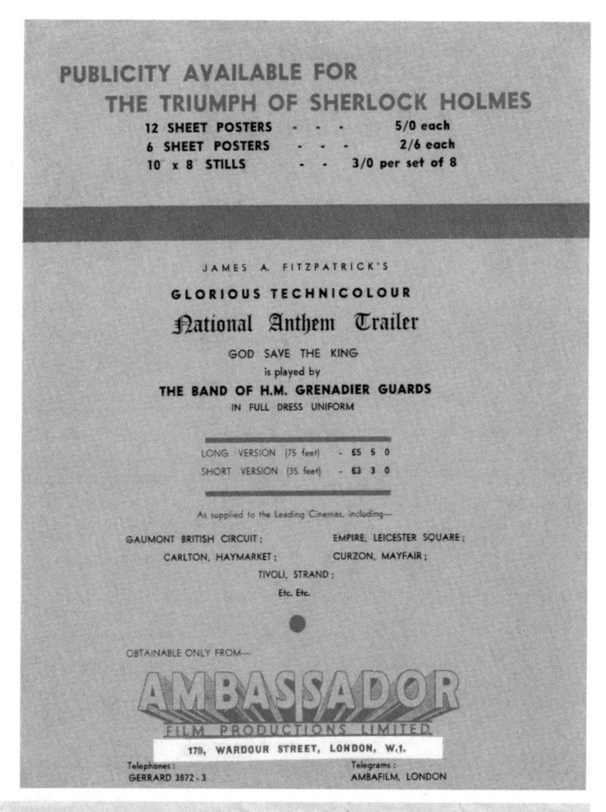

PUBLICITY AVAILABLE FOR
THE TRIUMPH OF SHERLOCK HOLMES

12 SHEET POSTERS - - -	5/0 each
6 SHEET POSTERS - - -	2/6 each
10" x 8" STILLS - -	3/0 per set of 8

JAMES A. FITZPATRICK'S
GLORIOUS TECHNICOLOUR
National Anthem Trailer
GOD SAVE THE KING
is played by
THE BAND OF H.M. GRENADIER GUARDS
IN FULL DRESS UNIFORM

LONG VERSION (75 feet)	- £5 5 0
SHORT VERSION (35 feet)	- £3 3 0

As supplied to the Leading Cinemas, including—
GAUMONT BRITISH CIRCUIT; EMPIRE, LEICESTER SQUARE;
CARLTON, HAYMARKET; CURZON, MAYFAIR;
TIVOLI, STRAND;
Etc. Etc.

OBTAINABLE ONLY FROM—
AMBASSADOR
FILM PRODUCTIONS LIMITED
179, WARDOUR STREET, LONDON, W.1.
Telephones: GERRARD 3872-3
Telegrams: AMBAFILM, LONDON

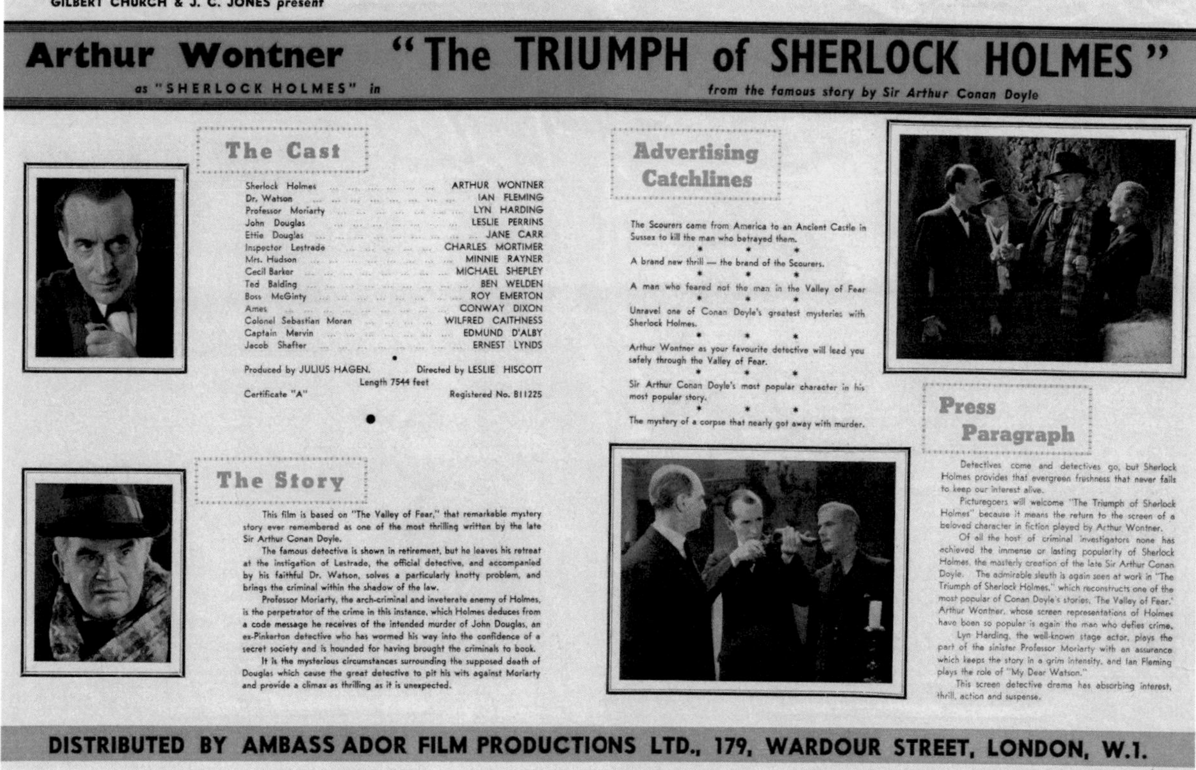

GILBERT CHURCH & J. C. JONES present
Arthur Wontner as "SHERLOCK HOLMES" in "The TRIUMPH of SHERLOCK HOLMES"
from the famous story by Sir Arthur Conan Doyle

The Cast

Sherlock Holmes	ARTHUR WONTNER
Dr. Watson	IAN FLEMING
Professor Moriarty	LYN HARDING
John Douglas	LESLIE PERRINS
Ettie Douglas	JANE CARR
Inspector Lestrade	CHARLES MORTIMER
Mrs. Hudson	MINNIE RAYNER
Cecil Barker	MICHAEL SHEPLEY
Ted Balding	BEN WELDEN
Boss McGinty	ROY EMERTON
Ames	CONWAY DIXON
Colonel Sebastian Moran	WILFRED CAITHNESS
Captain Mervin	EDMUND D'ALBY
Jacob Shafter	ERNEST LYNDS

Produced by JULIUS HAGEN. Directed by LESLIE HISCOTT
Length 7544 feet
Certificate "A" Registered No. B11225

The Story

This film is based on "The Valley of Fear," that remarkable mystery story ever remembered as one of the most thrilling written by the late Sir Arthur Conan Doyle.

The famous detective is shown in retirement, but he leaves his retreat at the instigation of Lestrade, the official detective, and accompanied by his faithful Dr. Watson, solves a particularly knotty problem, and brings the criminal within the shadow of the law.

Professor Moriarty, the arch-criminal and inveterate enemy of Holmes, is the perpetrator of the crime in this instance, which Holmes deduces from a code message he receives of the intended murder of John Douglas, an ex-Pinkerton detective who has wormed his way into the confidence of a secret society and is hounded for having brought the criminals to book.

It is the mysterious circumstances surrounding the supposed death of Douglas which cause the great detective to pit his wits against Moriarty and provide a climax as thrilling as it is unexpected.

Advertising Catchlines

The Scourers came from America to an Ancient Castle in Sussex to kill the man who betrayed them.

* * *

A brand new thrill — the brand of the Scourers.

* * *

A man who feared not the man in the Valley of Fear

* * *

Unravel one of Conan Doyle's greatest mysteries with Sherlock Holmes.

* * *

Arthur Wontner as your favourite detective will lead you safely through the Valley of Fear.

* * *

Sir Arthur Conan Doyle's most popular character in his most popular story.

* * *

The mystery of a corpse that nearly got away with murder.

Press Paragraph

Detectives come and detectives go, but Sherlock Holmes provides that evergreen freshness that never fails to keep our interest alive.

Picturegoers will welcome "The Triumph of Sherlock Holmes" because it means the return to the screen of a beloved character in fiction played by Arthur Wontner.

Of all the host of criminal investigators none has achieved the immense or lasting popularity of Sherlock Holmes, the masterly creation of the late Sir Arthur Conan Doyle. The admirable sleuth is again seen at work in "The Triumph of Sherlock Holmes," which reconstructs one of the most popular of Conan Doyle's stories, 'The Valley of Fear.' Arthur Wontner, whose screen representations of Holmes have been so popular is again the man who defies crime.

Lyn Harding, the well-known stage actor, plays the part of the sinister Professor Moriarty with an assurance which keeps the story in a grim intensity, and Ian Fleming plays the role of "My Dear Watson."

This screen detective drama has absorbing interest, thrill, action and suspense.

DISTRIBUTED BY AMBASS ADOR FILM PRODUCTIONS LTD., 179, WARDOUR STREET, LONDON, W.1.

Left:
Fatal Hour (February 1931)
AKA “The Sleeping Cardinal”
US 11 x 14 in (28 x 36 cm)

The Missing Rembrandt (March 1932)
US 27 x 41 in (69 x 104 cm)

The Sign of Four (August 1932)
US 11 x 14 in (28 x 36 cm)

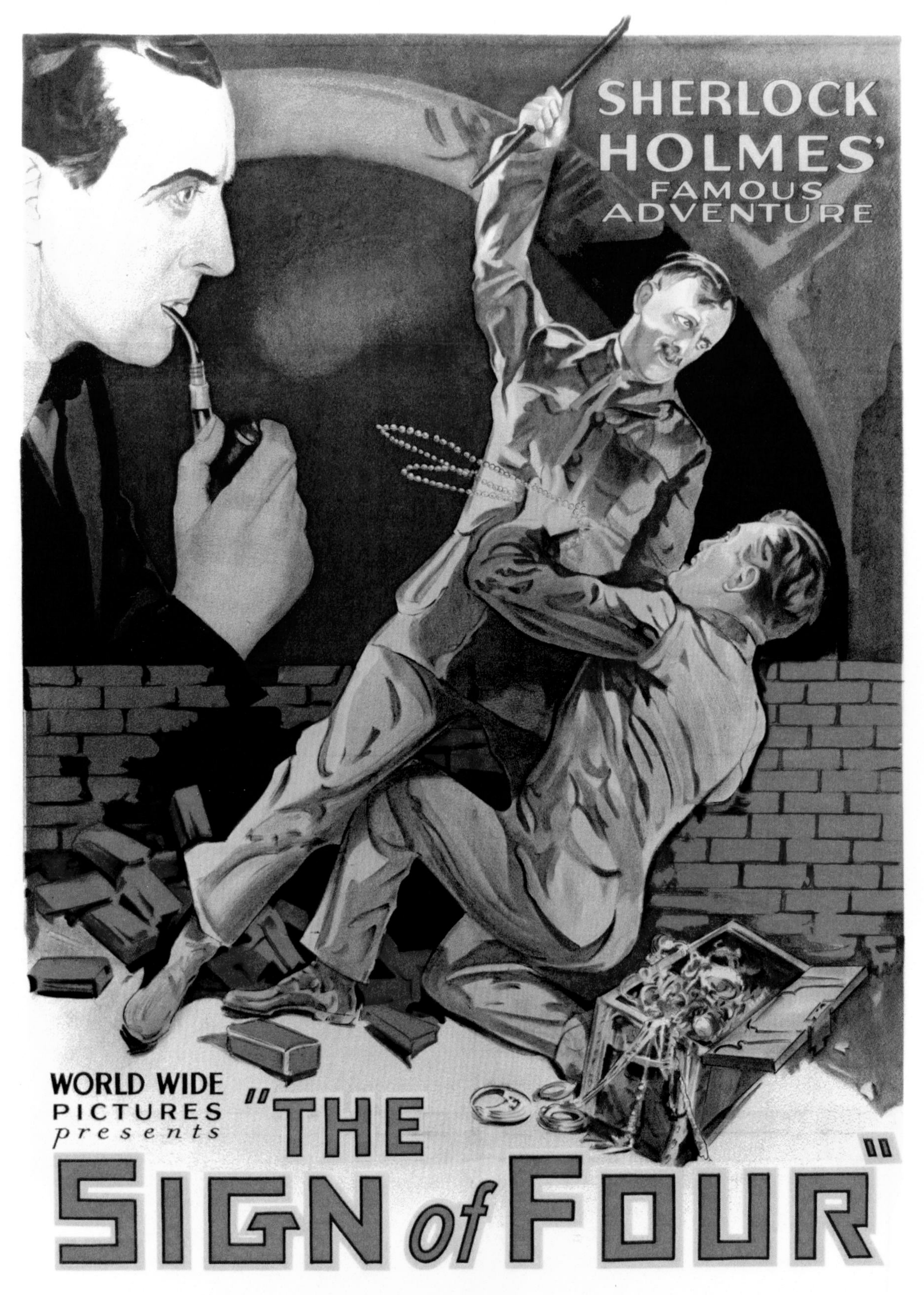

The Sign of Four (August 1932)
US 27 x 41 in (69 x 104 cm) "Style A"

The Sign of Four (August 1932)
US 27 x 41 in (69 x 104 cm) "Style B"

Murder At The Baskervilles was Wontner's final Holmes film.

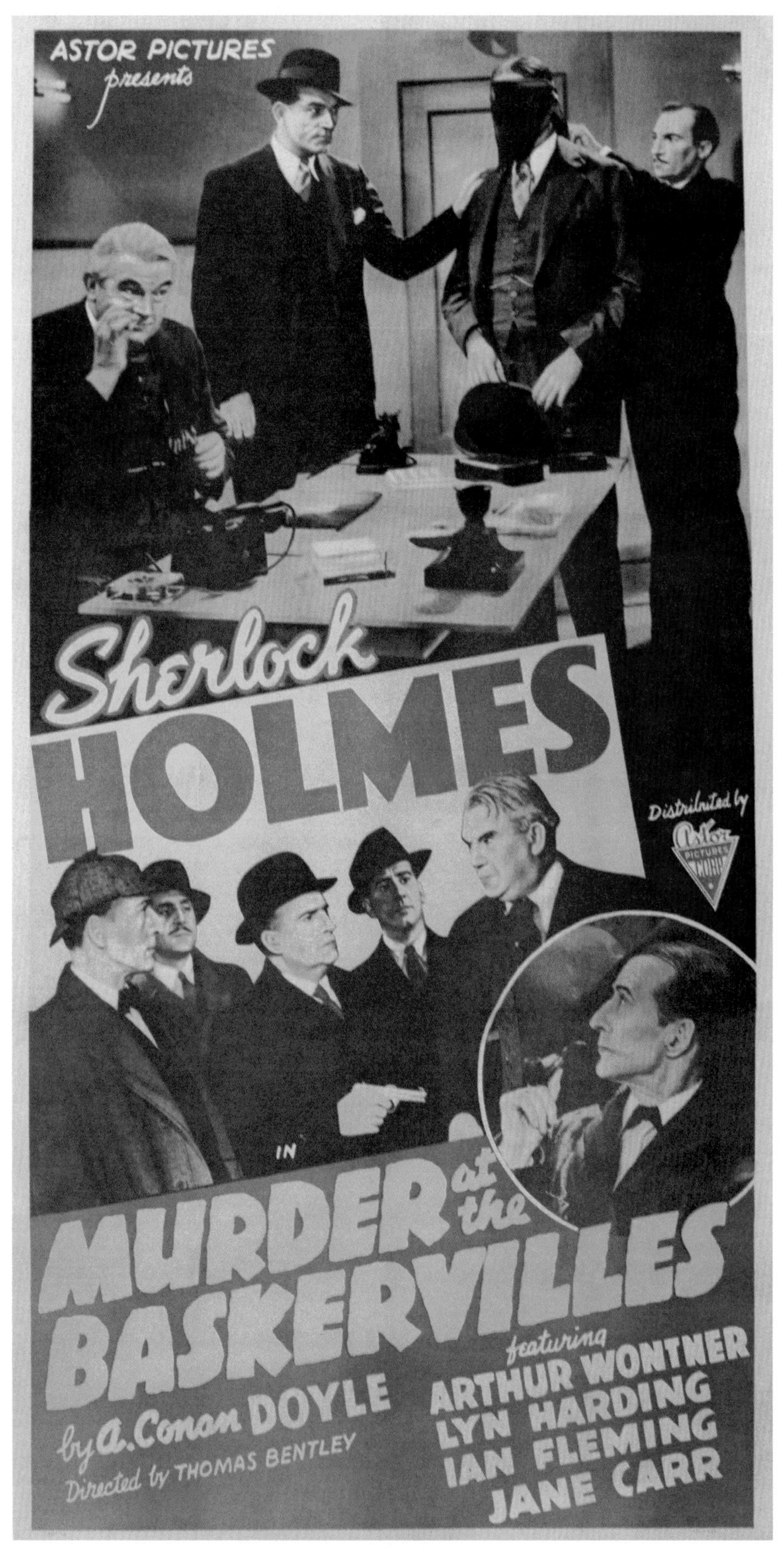

Murder at the Baskervilles (January 1937)
AKA "Silver Blaze"
US 41 x 81 in (104 x 206 cm)

Murder at the Baskervilles (January 1937)
US 11 x 14 in (28 x 36 cm)

While Arthur Wontner was the reigning Holmes, Reginald Owen, who, just a year earlier, portrayed Dr. Watson in *Sherlock Holmes* (1932), took on the lead role in Fox's *A Study in Scarlet* (1933), featuring Anna May Wong as Mrs. Pyke.

A Study in Scarlet (May 1933)
Sweeden 27½ x 39½ in (70 x 104 cm)

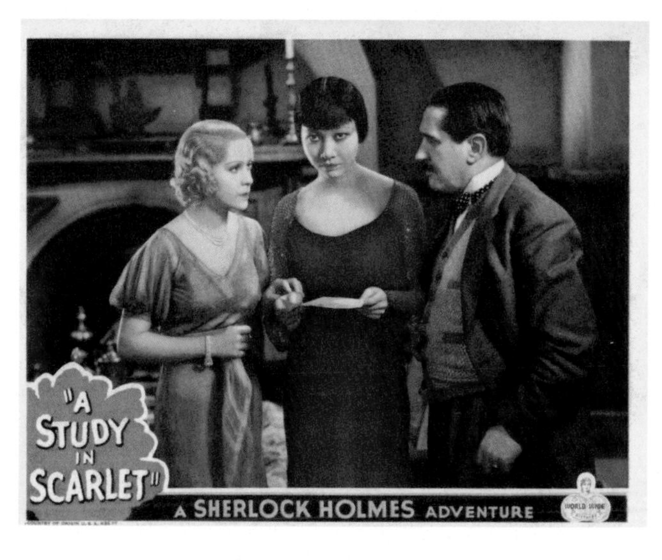

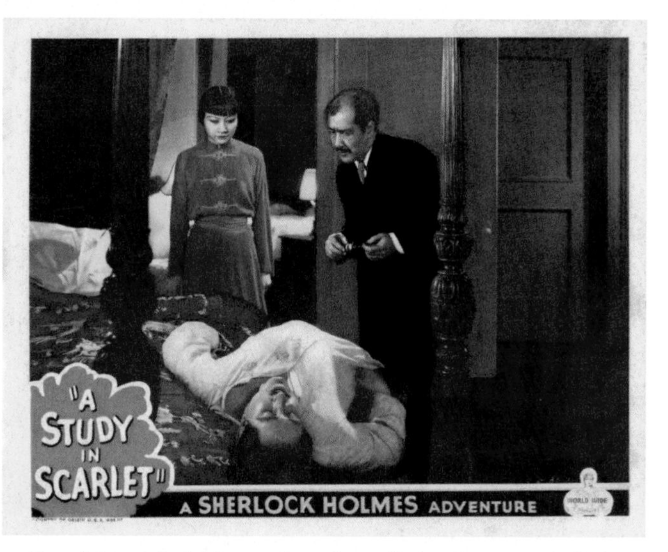

A Study in Scarlet (May 1933)
US 11 x 14 in (28 x 36 cm)

Six of the eight lobby card set from "A Study in Scarlet", three of which prominently feature fan favorite, Anna May Wong.

A Study in Scarlet (May 1933)
US 22 x 28 in (56 x 71 cm)
Type "A" & "B" ½ Sheet Posters

CAST

Sherlock Holmes	REGINALD OWEN
Mrs. Pyke	ANNA MAY WONG
Eileen Forrester	JUNE CLYDE
Merrydew	ALLAN DINEHART
John Stanford	JOHN WARBURTON
Dr. Watson	WARBURTON GAMBLE
Jabez Wilson	J. M. KERRIGAN
Lestrade	ALAN MOWBRAY
Mrs. Murphy	DORIS LLOYD
Will Swallow	BILLY BEVAN
Dolly	LEILA BENNETT
Baker	CECIL REYNOLDS
Capt. Pyke	WYNDHAM STANDING
Dearing	HALLIWELL HOBBES
Ah Yet	TETSU KOMAI
Mrs. Hudson	TEMPLE PIGOTT

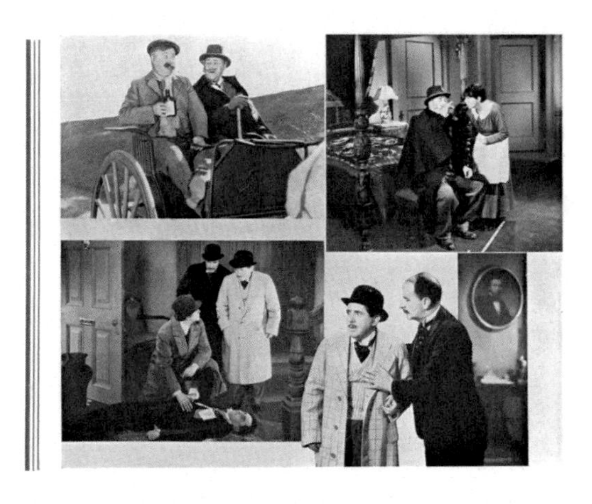

Programme: A Study in Scarlet
(May 1933)

1937 brought us two German "Sherlocks"... Bruno Güttner starred as Holmes in *The Hound of the Baskervilles* with Hans Albers, as a confidence man who impersonate Holmes and Watson. In a strange twist, according to some sources, these two films were actually found in Adolf Hitler's bunker by the Allies in 1945.

Sherlock Holmes (December 1937)
AKA "Two Merry Adventurers"
Germany 24 x 34 in (61 x 86 cm)

Left: The Hound of the Baskervilles (January 1937)
AKA "Der Hund Von Basterville"
Germany 36 x 55 in (91 x 140 cm)

Sherlock Holmes (December 1937)
AKA "Two Merry Adventurers"
Germany 38 x 55 in (97 x 140 cm)

Sherlock Holmes (December 1937)
AKA "Two Merry Adventurers"
Germany 38 x 55 in (97 x 140 cm)

Holmes's impact on popular culture was never more evident than it was in the early 1930s to the early 1940s. A flurry of "parody" films were released during this period, typically starring prominent comedy actors of the day. Stars such as The Marx Brothers, Laurel and Hardy, Abbott and Costello, Charlie McCarthy and even Gracie Allen took a turn in Sherlock's shoes.

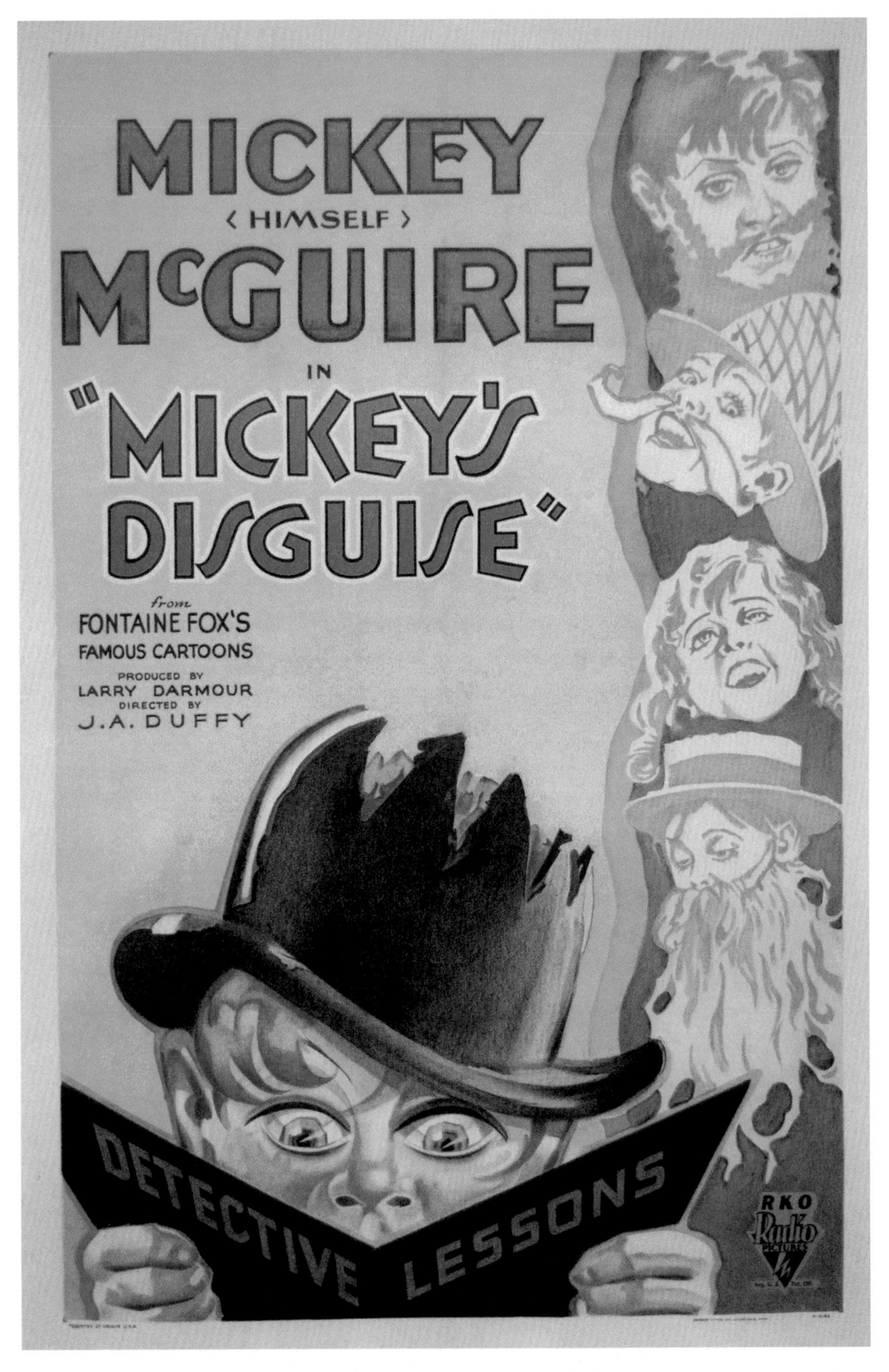

Mickey's Disguise (July 1933)
US 27 x 41 in (69 x 104 cm)

Duck Soup - Tha Marx Brothers
Released: November 1933
Harpo Marx (left) wearing a deerstalker cap as "Pinky" the detective.

Lost in Limehouse
Released: November 1933
Olaf Hytten (right) as "Sheerluck Jones".

The Radio Murder Mystery
Released: March 1933
Richard Gordon, the radio voice of Sherlock Holmes

The Three Stooges - Horse Collars (January 1935)
US 11 x 14 in (28 x 36 cm)

*Image courtesy of "The Stoogeum"
www.Stoogeum.com

The Gracie Allen Murder Case (June 1939)
US 11 x 14 in (28 x 36 cm)

Super-Sleuth (July 1937)
US 11 x 14 in (28 x 36 cm)

Death of A Champion (August 1939)
US 11 x 14 in (28 x 36 cm)

Charlie McCarthy, Detective (December 1939)
US 11 x 14 in (28 x 36 cm)

Charlie McCarthy, Detective (December 1939)
US 8 x 10 in (20 x 25 cm)

Charlie McCarthy, Detective (December 1939)
US 27 x 41 in (69 x 104 cm)

Who Done It? (November 1942)
US 27 x 41 in (69 x 104 cm)

The Big Noise (October 1944)
US 27 x 41 in (69 x 104 cm)

The Universal Years

A new chapter in the life of Sherlock started in 1939 when, hot on the heels of *Son of Frankenstein*, 47-year old Basil Rathbone picked up the pipe for the first time and took on what would become his alter-ego for the next seven years and beyond. Along with Nigel Bruce as Dr. John Watson, the duo worked in 14 Holmes films, and in doing so, became the best known portrayal of Conan Doyle's greatest creation.

The Hound of the Baskervilles (March 1939)
US 11 x 14 in (28 x 36 cm)

The Hound of the Baskervilles (March 1939)
US 11 x 14 in (28 x 36 cm)

BASIL RATHBONE
IN
SHERLOCK HOMES
MAKE-UP DEPT.

The Adventures of Sherlock Holmes (September 1939)
Mexico 13 x 17 in (33 x 43 cm)

Left:
Fox Studios Make-Up Department
Concept Drawing of Holmes in Disguise for
The Adventures of Sherlock Holmes

The Adventures of Sherlock Holmes (September 1939)
US 14 x 36 in (36 x 91 cm)

Sherlock Holmes and The Voice of Terror was released in the United States on September 18, 1942 and was based on Sir Arthur Conan Doyle's book *His Last Bow*.

The Voice of Terror is, in fact, a Nazi radio announcer preaching the propaganda of the Third Reich, carrying out a campaign of fear against the Brits. After numerous attacks by Germany on several key targets, Sir Evan Barham (Reginald Denny) announces to the members of the Intelligence Inner Council that he has asked Sherlock Holmes to meet with them. The council protests the idea of bringing a private citizen into their government business. Nonetheless, Holmes is on the case.

While strategizing their next move, a dying man (Robert Barron) staggers into Baker Street with a knife in his back. He immediately falls to the floor, and with his dying breath says the name "Christopher". Holmes takes the incident as a warning message for him, but nonetheless, announces that they must get to a rather shady part of London known as Limehouse. The two enter a rowdy tavern in search of "Kitty" (Evelyn Ankers), the girlfriend of the man (Gavin) who was just murdered at Holmes' flat. They break the bad news to the young lady, who is in disbelief that her beau could be dead. Holmes engages Kitty to help discover the meaning of "Christopher" and in order to find answers she shames the seedy tavern patrons into helping her.

Holmes returns to the Intelligence Inner Council and, as their meeting is getting underway, the Nazi Voice of Terror broadcasts another message: their latest act of sabotage was to burn down a building which was housing aircraft and other military assets. Returning to their session, Holmes reveals to the group that he believes the Voice of Terror messages are pre-recorded and originate in England. The council members scoff at the idea that the messages are being recorded in England, however. Holmes explains that he has discovered that on regular intervals a Nazi spy is picking up plans, maps and secret military information, along with the Voice of Terror recordings, which would later be broadcast from Germany. Kitty arrives on the scene to give a message to Holmes. Upon hearing the message, Holmes announces that he must leave immediately, but is unable to tell them where he is going.

After another Voice of Terror broadcast, the council determines that the Nazis will be invading England's north coast. Holmes thinks differently and tells the group that the invasion will be on the south coast. After receiving a call from Downing Street, Sir Evan informs the council that they must follow Holmes.

Holmes' conclusion was of course correct, and they find and arrest a group of Nazis, in full German uniform. Holmes then announces that Sir Evan was in fact a German imposter who was passing along secrets. The Nazi contingent feels that they still have the upper hand, and that their forces will be soon invading England. However, their hopes are quashed by the sound of British aircraft returning from successfully wiping out the German invasion.

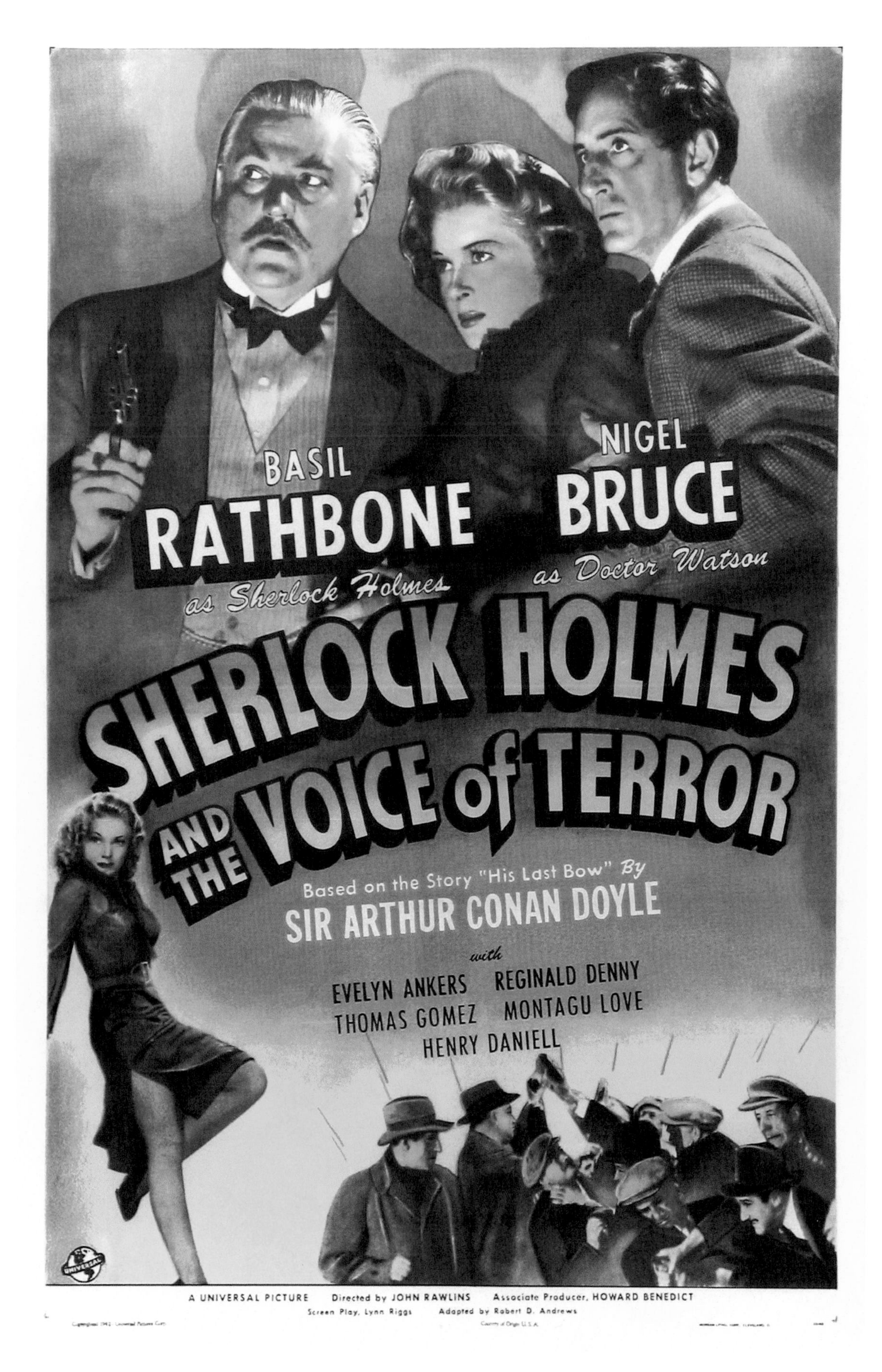

Sherlock Holmes and The Voice of Terror (September 1942)
US 27 x 41 in (69 x 104 cm)

BASIL
RATHBONE
as Sherlock Holmes
Nigel BRUCE
as Doctor Watson
in
SHERLOCK HOLMES
AND THE VOICE of TERROR
Based on the Story "His Last Bow" by
SIR ARTHUR CONAN DOYLE
with
EVELYN ANKERS REGINALD DENNY
THOMAS GOMEZ MONTAGU LOVE
HENRY DANIELL

BASIL
RATHBONE
as Sherlock Holmes
Nigel BRUCE
as Doctor Watson
SHERLOCK HOLMES
AND THE VOICE of TERROR
A UNIVERSAL PICTURE

BASIL
RATHBONE
as Sherlock Holmes
Nigel BRUCE
as Doctor Watson
SHERLOCK HOLMES
AND THE VOICE of TERROR
A UNIVERSAL PICTURE

BASIL
RATHBONE
as Sherlock Holmes
Nigel BRUCE
as Doctor Watson
SHERLOCK HOLMES
AND THE VOICE of TERROR
A UNIVERSAL PICTURE

BASIL
RATHBONE
as Sherlock Holmes
Nigel BRUCE
as Doctor Watson
SHERLOCK HOLMES
AND THE VOICE of TERROR
A UNIVERSAL PICTURE

BASIL
RATHBONE
as Sherlock Holmes
Nigel BRUCE
as Doctor Watson
SHERLOCK HOLMES
AND THE VOICE of TERROR
A UNIVERSAL PICTURE

BASIL
RATHBONE
as Sherlock Holmes
Nigel BRUCE
as Doctor Watson
SHERLOCK HOLMES
AND THE VOICE of TERROR
A UNIVERSAL PICTURE

BASIL
RATHBONE
as Sherlock Holmes
Nigel BRUCE
as Doctor Watson
SHERLOCK HOLMES
AND THE VOICE of TERROR
A UNIVERSAL PICTURE

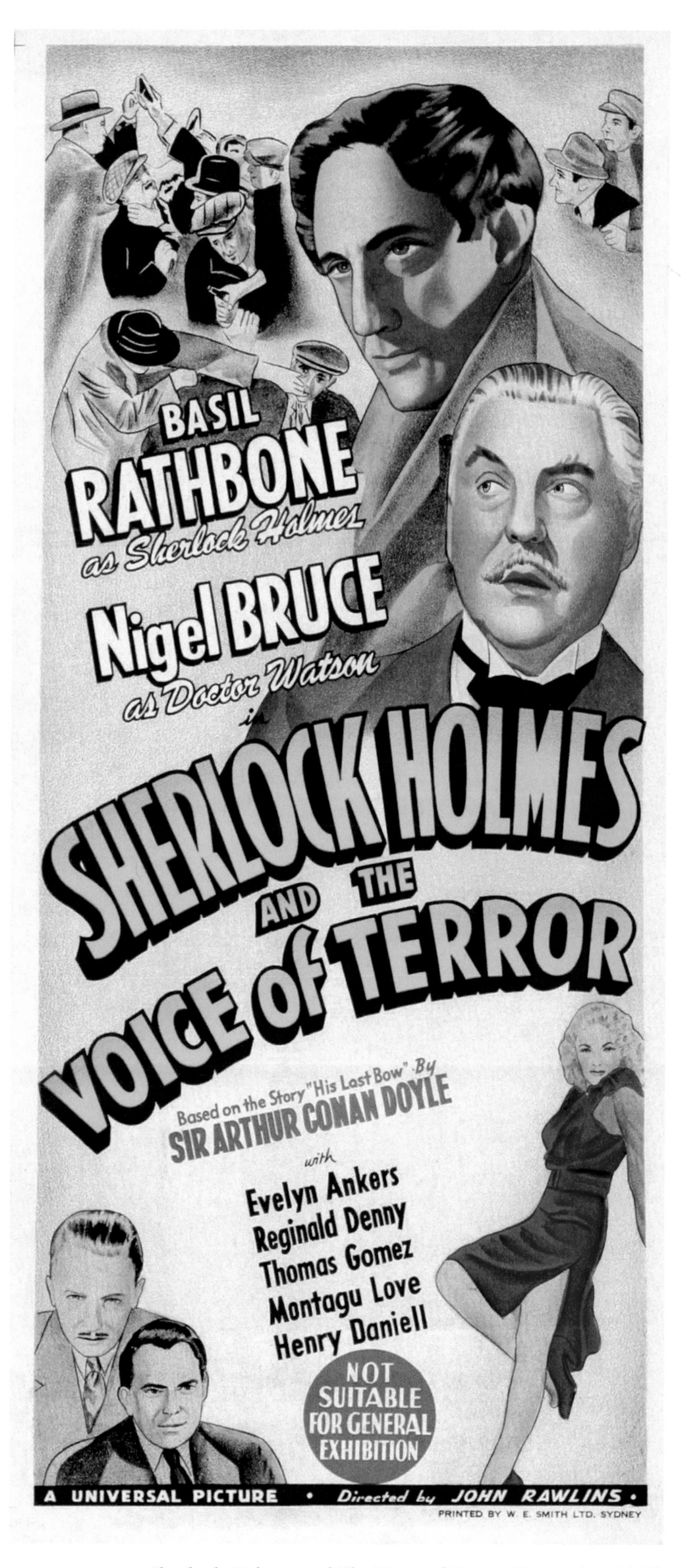

Sherlock Holmes and The Voice of Terror (September 1942)
Australia 13 x 30 in (33 x 84 cm)

Left:
Sherlock Holmes and The Voice of Terror (September 1942)
US 11 x 14 in (28 x 36 cm)

The Secret Weapon was released February 12th, 1943, and starts out in a tavern, where an in-disguise Holmes attempts to sell books to two German agents. The transaction is, in fact, a ruse to pass along plans for a covert operation in support of the fatherland. Holmes plays along as part of his larger plan. Dressed as an elderly book seller, he leaves the two agents and walks across the street to meet with a contact (William Post Jr. as Dr. Franz Tobel), whom he will ultimately smuggle out of the country and back to England in a waiting RAF plane.

Dr. Tobel is a Swiss scientist who has agreed to provide the Brits with his new bomb guidance system. After an eventful evening that includes Tobel visiting a young lady and subsequently getting mugged on the way home, the trio heads out the next morning to witness a test of the doctor's invention. Just hours after the successful test run, Tobel goes missing, but not before he divides his invention into four pieces, leaving each of the parts with four separate scientists for safekeeping.

Holmes soon discovers that Professor Moriarty (Lionel Atwill) was in fact the kidnapper, working on a plan to sell Tobel's invention to the Nazis. Although Moriarty stole the code that would lead him to the four scientists in possession of the guidance system, Holmes is able to uncover a copy of the code. With Holmes' nemesis a few steps ahead of him, the first three scientists fall victim to the professor's henchmen.

Fortunately, Holmes' superior intellect allows him to break the code ahead of Moriarty, and he is able to reach, and take the place of, the fourth scientist ahead of the killer's arrival. Holmes (in disguise) is taken back to the kidnapper's lair, and Moriarty soon discovers that he has been tricked by Holmes, who does not possess the vital final piece of the explosive puzzle.

Of course Sherlock is one step ahead of Moriarty, and he was able to lead Scotland Yard to his location, to save the day. Moriarty escapes through a secret passage, but we soon hear him scream, followed by Holmes commenting on the fact that someone may have left a trap door open, through which Moriarty fell to his death...or did he?

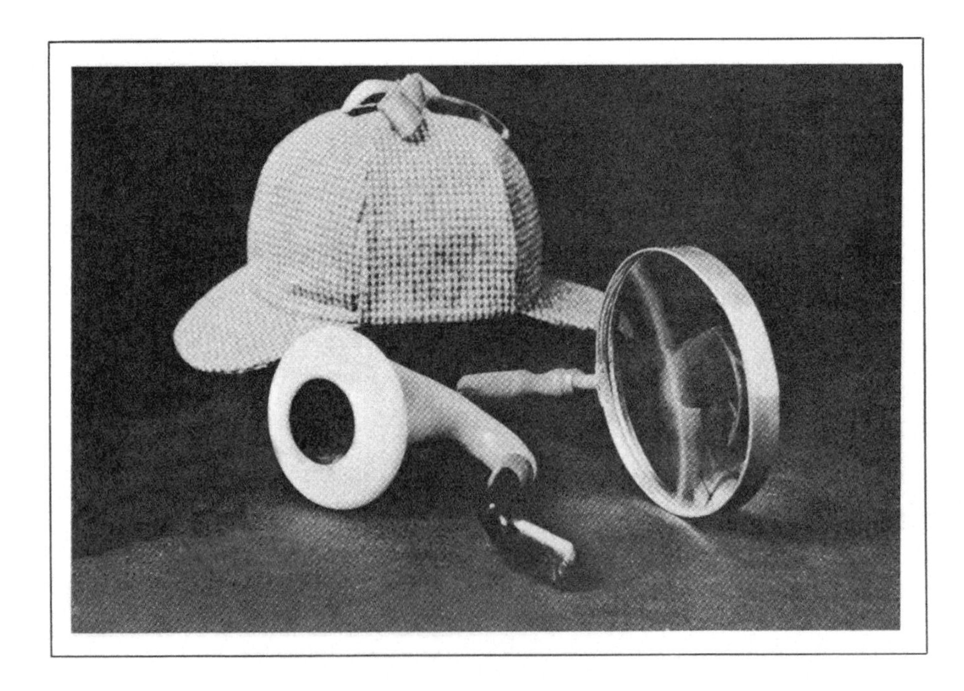

Sherlock Holmes and The Secret Weapon (February 1943)
US 27 x 41 in (69 x 104 cm)

BASIL
RATHBONE
as Sherlock Holmes
NIGEL
BRUCE
as Doctor Watson
in
SHERLOCK HOLMES
AND THE Secret Weapon
Based on the Story "THE DANCING MEN" by
SIR ARTHUR CONAN DOYLE
LIONEL ATWILL
as Moriarty
KAAREN VERNE
WILLIAM POST, Jr.
DENNIS HOEY

SHERLOCK HOLMES
AND THE Secret Weapon
A UNIVERSAL PICTURE

SHERLOCK HOLMES
AND THE Secret Weapon
A UNIVERSAL PICTURE

SHERLOCK HOLMES
AND THE Secret Weapon
A UNIVERSAL PICTURE

SHERLOCK HOLMES
AND THE Secret Weapon
A UNIVERSAL PICTURE

SHERLOCK HOLMES
AND THE Secret Weapon
A UNIVERSAL PICTURE

SHERLOCK HOLMES
AND THE Secret Weapon
A UNIVERSAL PICTURE

SHERLOCK HOLMES
AND THE Secret Weapon
A UNIVERSAL PICTURE

Sherlock Holmes and The Secret Weapon (February 1943)
Sweden 27 x 39 in (69 x 99 cm)

Left:
Sherlock Holmes and The Secret Weapon (February 1943)
US 11 x 14 in (28 x 36 cm)

Sherlock Holmes and The Secret Weapon - Realart Re-Release (December 1948)
US 14 x 36 in (36 x 91 cm)

Sherlock Holmes and The Secret Weapon - Realart Re-Release (December 1948)
US 27 x 41 in (69 x 104 cm)

Sherlock Holmes and The Secret Weapon (February 1943)
US 22 x 28 in (56 x 71 cm)
"A" and "B" Styles - Realart Re-release: 1948

Sherlock Holmes and The Secret Weapon February 1943
Australia 13 x 30 in (33 x 76 cm)

Sherlock Holmes in Washington was released in the U.S. on April 30, 1943 and was based on an original story by Betram Millhauser. It was directed by Roy William Neill.

Departing from the London terminal of Transatlantic Airlines, Sir Henry Marchmon (Gilbert Emery) is surrounded by reporters pressing him for details about his trip.

Ultimately landing in New York, Sir Henry boards a Washington-bound train that carries fellow passengers William Easter (Henry Daniell) John Grayson (Gerald Hamer), both of which were on his London flight. Grayson is reading a newspaper with a front page story titled "Ace British Diplomat Enroute to Washington". A few minutes later we find Easter and two associates discussing who may be carrying a secret government document, and after discounting Sir Henry, they come to the conclusion that Grayson must be the man they are looking for. They quickly devise a plan to abduct Grayson to retrieve the document.

Grayson notices Easter eyeing him suspiciously and becomes alarmed that foul play is at hand. Hoping to head off any issues, Grayson strikes up a conversation with fellow passenger Senator Henry Babcock (Thurston Hall), and also assists a young lady, Nancy Partridge (Marjorie Lord), by lighting her cigarette, and subsequently slipping a book of matches into her purse.

After creating a small diversion, Easter and company manage to grab Grayson. News of the disappearance of a British subject garners a lot of attention in the media, and just as Holmes and Watson are listening to a radio news broadcast of the disappearance, they receive an unannounced visit from Mr. Ahrens (Holmes Herbert) who implores Holmes, on behalf of the British government, to take the case. It seems that Grayson was actually Alfred Pettibone, an undercover operative who was carrying an important government document which must not fall into enemy hands.

Before heading off to Washington, Holmes decides to search Pettibone's home. Holmes discovers clues that lead him to believe that Grayson/Pettibone reduced the documents to microfilm and concealed them in a book of matches. While leaving the residence, the pair narrowly escape injury when a large brick falls from the roof. It is now clear that Pettibone's abductors are aware that Holmes is on the case.

Holmes and Watson are off to America to meet with government agent Lang (Gavin Muir) and Detective Lt. Grogan (Edmund MacDonald) of the Washington police. On the drive from the airport Holmes thanks Lang for his cablegram and invitation to stay at the Hotel Metropole, to which Lang clarifies that he didn't send the cable and had expected the two to stay at the embassy.

The four are reviewing the case when a porter shows up with what is supposed to be Holmes' steamer trunk. Knowing it wasn't his trunk, they carefully look inside, only to find a very dead Grayson. Holmes surmises that the killers are simply trying to throw him off track and make him think that they already have the secret government papers.

Holmes returns to the scene of the crime, looking for clues in the club car, finding that it had been ransacked. Nevertheless, Holmes reconstructs the scene, discovering that Grayson had lit Miss Partridge's cigarette...a seemingly important point.

After a visit to the police lab, Holmes surmises that the blanket that Grayson was wrapped in came from an antique store, so they set out on an expedition to find the right shop. In short order, Holmes finds the right place, and is able to catch the culprits who unwittingly have the microfilm in hand.

Sherlock Holmes in (April 1943)
US 27 x 41 in (69 x 104 cm)

BASIL
RATHBONE
as Sherlock Holmes
NIGEL
BRUCE
as Doctor Watson
SHERLOCK HOLMES
IN WASHINGTON
Based on the characters created by
SIR ARTHUR CONAN DOYLE
with
MARJORIE LORD JOHN ARCHER DON TERRY
GEORGE ZUCCO HENRY DANIELL EDMUND MacDONALD

BASIL RATHBONE and NIGEL BRUCE
as Sherlock Holmes as Doctor Watson
in
SHERLOCK HOLMES
IN WASHINGTON
A UNIVERSAL PICTURE

BASIL RATHBONE and NIGEL BRUCE
as Sherlock Holmes as Doctor Watson
in
SHERLOCK HOLMES
IN WASHINGTON
A UNIVERSAL PICTURE

BASIL RATHBONE and NIGEL BRUCE
as Sherlock Holmes as Doctor Watson
in
SHERLOCK HOLMES
IN WASHINGTON
A UNIVERSAL PICTURE

BASIL RATHBONE and NIGEL BRUCE
as Sherlock Holmes as Doctor Watson
in
SHERLOCK HOLMES
IN WASHINGTON
A UNIVERSAL PICTURE

BASIL RATHBONE and NIGEL BRUCE
as Sherlock Holmes as Doctor Watson
in
SHERLOCK HOLMES
IN WASHINGTON
A UNIVERSAL PICTURE

BASIL RATHBONE and NIGEL BRUCE
as Sherlock Holmes as Doctor Watson
in
SHERLOCK HOLMES
IN WASHINGTON
A UNIVERSAL PICTURE

BASIL RATHBONE and NIGEL BRUCE
as Sherlock Holmes as Doctor Watson
in
SHERLOCK HOLMES
IN WASHINGTON
A UNIVERSAL PICTURE

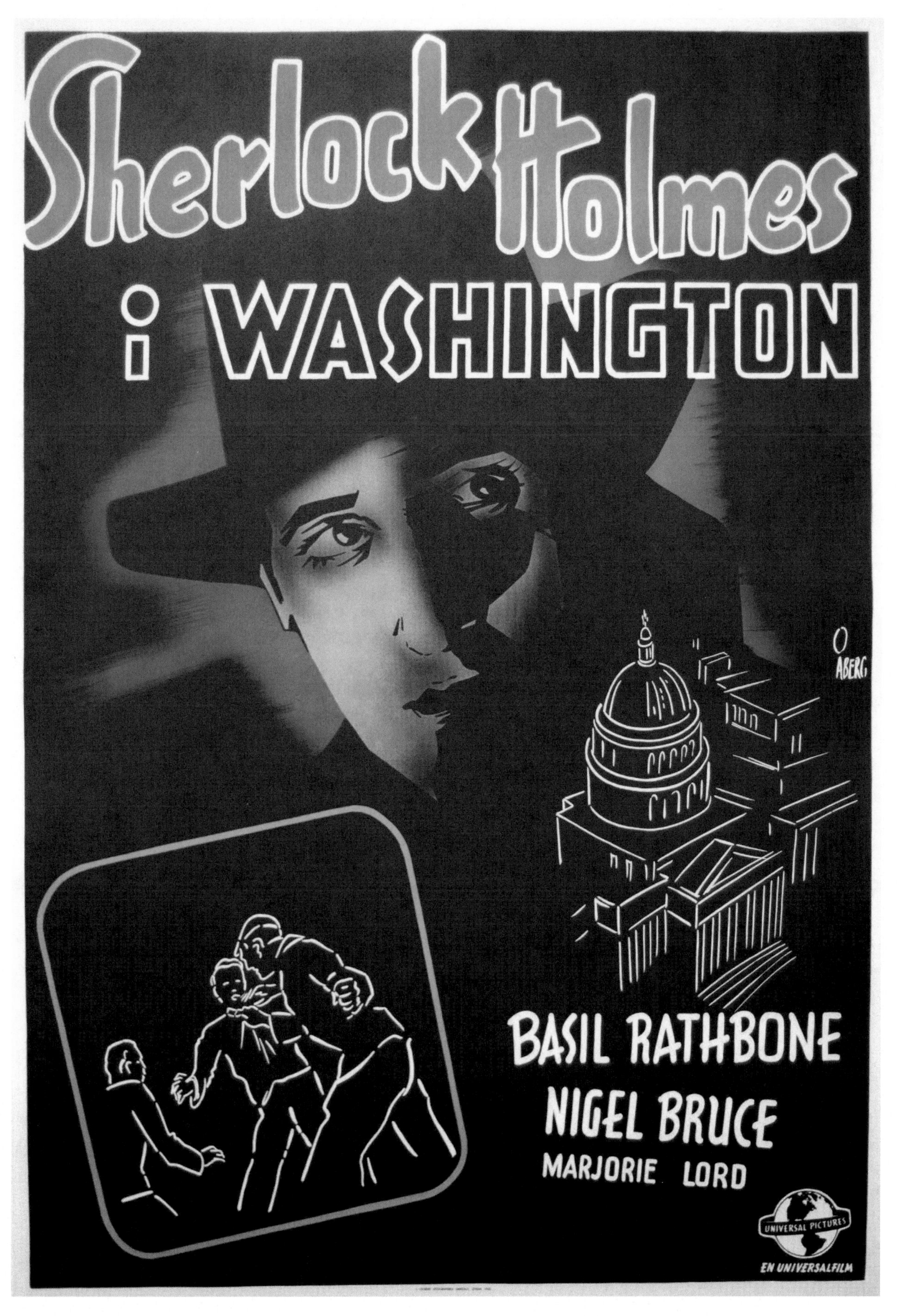

Sherlock Holmes in Washington (April 1943)
Sweden 27½ x 39½ in (70 x 100 cm)

Left:
Sherlock Holmes in Washington (April 1943)
US 11 x 14 in (28 x 36 cm)

Sherlock Holmes Faces Death was released in the U.S. on September 17, 1943. Based on a screenplay by Betram Millhauser, was produced and directed by Roy William Neill.

The story starts at the Rat and the Raven tavern, an establishment frequented by sailors (including a young Peter Lawford in an early uncredited role), and home to the tavern's namesake "Charlie" the raven. When Charlie starts behaving oddly at the sight of blood on a patron, the proprietor (Harold De Becker) explains that his strange behavior was a result of him heralding from Musgrave Manor, a local haunted mansion that has recently been converted to a convalescing home for troubled ex-military officers.

We find Watson working at the manor as a short-term staff member. While doing some research in the library, his assistant Dr. Sexton (Arthur Margetson), staggers into the room with a knife wound on his neck. Sexton explains to Watson and Brunton, the butler (Halliwell Hobbes) that he was attacked outside the door by an unseen assailant.

Returning to Baker Street the next morning, Watson tells Holmes about the past evenings events and the two are shortly en route back to the manor to investigate the crime. Upon their arrival, Holmes spots a large pile of leaves raked in front of a greenhouse door, which he finds peculiar. As the pair investigate, they find Jeffrey Musgrave (Frederick Worlock) buried under the leaves.

Inspector Lestrade (Dennis Hoey) is also at the manor on the case when Holmes and Watson enter the room and inform Phillip Musgrave (Gavin Muir) about finding his older brother dead.

The next day Phillip Musgrave goes missing, only to be found dead in the trunk of his sister Sally's (Hillary Brooke) car. Lestrade is convinced that Alfred Brunton is the killer, despite arresting Capt. Pat Vickery (Milburn Stone) a day earlier for the same crime. Lestrade is proven wrong on both counts, as Vickery was in jail when Phillip was killed and Brunton is subsequently found dead in a crypt beneath the manor.

Holmes reveals that Brunton may have written the name of his killer on the floor in his own blood and sets a plan in motion to catch the killer. Holmes supposedly leaves the manor to retrieve chemicals from his residence that will reveal the faint writing.

After a series of distractions, we next see someone approaching the writing on the floor, and as they reach for it, Holmes grabs the man's arm. Holmes then reveals that there was, in fact, no writing and that he created the ruse to mislead the killer (revealed as Dr. Sexton) whom he knew would return to erase the incriminating handwriting. A struggle ensues and the killer manages to take Holmes' gun. While being held at gunpoint, Holmes provokes Sexton into confessing to the murders. Sexton then shoots Holmes (who drops to the floor) and heads up the stairs to escape.

Rather than make his escape, Sexton finds Watson, Lestrade and others waiting to arrest him. An uninjured Holmes emerges from the lower level, confirming that everyone had heard the confession.

Holmes wraps the scene by apologizing to Sexton for making such a predictable move, - in loading his gun with blanks - which rubs salt in the wound for Sexton who fell for the ploy, hook, line and sinker.

Sherlock Holmes Faces Death (September 1943)
US 27 x 41 in (69 x 104 cm)

Basil
RATHBONE
as Sherlock Holmes
Nigel BRUCE
as Doctor Watson
Sherlock Holmes
FACES DEATH
with
HILLARY BROOKE MILBURN STONE
DENNIS HOEY ARTHUR MARGETSON
MARY GORDON HALLIWELL HOBBES

RATHBONE BRUCE
Sherlock Holmes FACES DEATH
A UNIVERSAL PICTURE

RATHBONE BRUCE
Sherlock Holmes FACES DEATH
A UNIVERSAL PICTURE

RATHBONE BRUCE
Sherlock Holmes FACES DEATH
A UNIVERSAL PICTURE

RATHBONE BRUCE
Sherlock Holmes FACES DEATH
A UNIVERSAL PICTURE

RATHBONE BRUCE
Sherlock Holmes FACES DEATH
A UNIVERSAL PICTURE

RATHBONE BRUCE
Sherlock Holmes FACES DEATH
A UNIVERSAL PICTURE

RATHBONE BRUCE
Sherlock Holmes FACES DEATH
A UNIVERSAL PICTURE

Sherlock Holmes Faces Death (September 1943)
Sweden 27 x 39 in (69 x 99 cm)

Sherlock Holmes Faces Death (September 1943)
Germany 23 x 33 in (59 x 84 cm)

Left:
Sherlock Holmes Faces Death (September 1943)
US 11 x 14 in (28 x 36 cm)

The *Spider Woman,* released in the U.S. on January 21, 1944, was an original story by writer Bertram Millhauser, loosely based on facets of several Conan Doyle works, including *The Sign of Four*, *The Final Problem*, *The Adventure of the Devil's Foot*, and *The Adventure of the Speckled Band.*

The film begins with a body crashing through a window, followed by newspapermen reading the headline "Another Pajama Suicide", dissolving to Holmes and Watson on a fishing holiday, when Holmes announces his retirement, due to a series of dizzy spells. Just moments later, Holmes faints and falls into a rushing river, ending the scene with the headlines announcing the death of Sherlock Holmes!

Watson and Mrs. Hudson (Mary Gordon) pack up books and journals for pickup by the British Museum. With regard to the melancholy mood, Mrs. Hudson remarks to Watson, "What can't be cured, must be endured". A postman comes to the door delivering a package for Sherlock Holmes. The elderly package carrier makes several derogatory comments about Holmes to Watson, who is ultimately pushed beyond his limit, and strikes the man down with a punch to the jaw. Chuckling, the man stands up, while pulling off a false moustache, revealing his true identity (to a very shaken up Watson) as none other than the late Sherlock Holmes himself!

Inspector Lestrade (Dennis Hoey) of Scotland Yard enters the room to find Holmes very much alive. Holmes explains that he felt it necessary to disappear in order to work the case of the recent string of murders, which he feels are the work of a "femme fatale". Both Watson and Lastrade feel that Holmes is off the mark believing the deaths are no more than suicide, since each victim was alone in a locked room. Holmes points out several suspicious similarities between the cases - each was fairly well off and they each "respond to the pleasures of a gaming table".

Holmes plants a story in the local newspapers about a fictional Indian Colonel, Rashnee Singh, who has a "well known devotion to the goddess of chance" and is visiting London to have surgeons restore his left arm which was injured in service to the empire.

Taking the bait, the female Moriarty, Adrea Spedding (Gale Sondergaard) meets Rashnee Singh at the Urban Casino to start spinning her web to ensnare her next prey. After meeting with Singh, Spedding suspects that Singh is a phony and he is actually Sherlock Holmes in disguise.

We next see Holmes asleep in bed and being approached by a very large spider. As the spider inches towards Holmes, its life is quickly ended by the point of a knife. With this failed attempt on Holmes' life, Spedding tries again with a visit to Holmes' Baker Street residence and a candy wrapper laced with the deadly poison, "devils foot". Fortunately, Holmes again cheats death and is more determined than ever to track down his adversary.

The overly intelligent Spedding devises a third and final plan to kill Holmes, luring him to a local carnival. While attempting to apprehend the femme fatale, Holmes is captured and finds himself a participant on the wrong side of the gun in a shooting gallery. After several attempts, Holmes is able to free himself, avoid being shot by Watson and snare the Spider Woman.

The Spider Woman (January 1944)
US 27 x 41 in (69 x 104 cm)

MISTRESS OF MURDER!
Basil RATHBONE
as Sherlock Holmes
Nigel BRUCE
as Doctor Watson
in
SPIDER WOMAN
Based on a story by SIR ARTHUR CONAN DOYLE
with
DENNIS HOEY VERNON DOWNING MARY GORDON
and
GALE SONDERGAARD
as the Spider Woman
A UNIVERSAL PICTURE

SPIDER WOMAN
A UNIVERSAL PICTURE

SPIDER WOMAN
A UNIVERSAL PICTURE

The Great
SPIDER WOMAN
A UNIVERSAL PICTURE

SPIDER WOMAN
A UNIVERSAL PICTURE

PUNCH AND JUDY
SPIDER WOMAN
A UNIVERSAL PICTURE

SPIDER WOMAN
A UNIVERSAL PICTURE

SPIDER WOMAN
A UNIVERSAL PICTURE

Left:
The Spider Woman (January 1944)
US 11 x 14 in (28 x 36 cm)

The Spider Woman (January 1944)
Australia 13 x 30 in (33 x 84 cm)

The Spider Woman (January 1944)
US 40 x 60 in (152 x 199 cm)

The Spider Woman (January 1944)
France 55 x 78 in (140 x 199 cm)

The Spider Woman (January 1944)
Italy 14 x 19 in (36 x 48 cm)

The Spider Woman (January 1944)
Belgium 14 x 21 in (36 x 53 cm)

The Scarlet Claw was released in the U.S. on May 26, 1944, and was based on an original story by Paul Gangelin and Brenda Weisberg, with a screenplay by Edmund L. Hartman and Roy William Neill (who also produced and directed the film).

Like many Holmes films, *Scarlet Claw* opens in a tavern where patrons are discussing a mysterious tolling of the church bell, as well as the fact that several sheep have been found dead with their throats torn out. Rumors of ghosts and monsters grow after Lady Penrose (Gertrude Astor) is found dead in the church, clutching the rope of the bell she had been tolling for help.

Lord Penrose (Paul Cavanagh, in his first of three Holmes feature roles) is informed of his wife's death while speaking at a symposium (attended by Holmes and Watson) of the Royal Canadian Occult Society. He was conveying his belief in the supernatural and its possible role in the recent brutal sheep killings. Penrose excused himself announcing that his wife had been found with her throat torn out, in the same manner as the sheep that had been recently killed. Holmes offered his assistance, but with the two gentlemen on opposite sides of the idea of the existence of a supernatural spirit at work, Penrose refused Holmes' offer.

As Holmes and Watson return to their hotel, the clerk gives Holmes a letter, a plea for his assistance from the late Lady Penrose. Holmes decides to take the case and announces to Watson that this is the first time he has been retained by a corpse.

The duo arrives at Primrose manor to find Lord Penrose in the parlor standing over his wife's body. With a quick look Holmes realizes that "Lady Penrose" was in fact Lillian Gentry, a famous American actress who vanished years earlier.

Watson heads to the local pub to mix with the locals in hopes of gathering information. Among the patrons is the Penroses' now-ex butler Drake (Ian Wolfe) and the local postman, "Potts" (Gerald Hamer), a friendly, chatty fellow with whom Watson strikes up a friendship.

As Watson engages with the townsfolk, Holmes heads out to the marshes where the killings have taken place, hoping to find clues to explain this monster which has the town in a frenzy. Holmes is soon being pursued by a glowing figure of a man, and he takes several shots at the approaching "monster". The ghostly figure runs away, but not before bumping into a tree branch which tears a piece from his clothing.

Holmes' investigation later reveals that the fabric left by the monster was a somewhat rare material used by a local shopkeeper to make shirts for local resident, Judge Brisson (Miles Mander). Brisson informs Holmes that he had donated a couple of his old shirts to a handyman, identified as a man named "Tanner". Tanner is later found to be a former actor by the name of Alastair Ramson, who was sentenced to prison for killing an actor in Lady Penrose's company five years earlier. Ransom was previously presumed dead, after attempting to escape his confinement.

Holmes develops a plan to catch the killer and sets things in motion at the local pub. He disguises himself as the pub owner Emile Journet (Arthur Hohl), who it is revealed, was a guard at the prison from which Ramson escaped. Holmes (as Journet) leaves on the pretext of going to church to say a prayer for his daughter Marie (Kay Harding), who was also murdered by Tanner. As Holmes is walking to the church, he is approached by local postman, Potts, who asks to walk with him. Potts quickly reveals himself to be Ramson and attempts to kill Holmes. Holmes' plan has worked perfectly and the two are surrounded by police and locals who are there to apprehend Tanner. As Tanner tries to flee, the real Journet comes across him, the two struggle, and Journet ultimately kills Tanner to avenge his daughter's death.

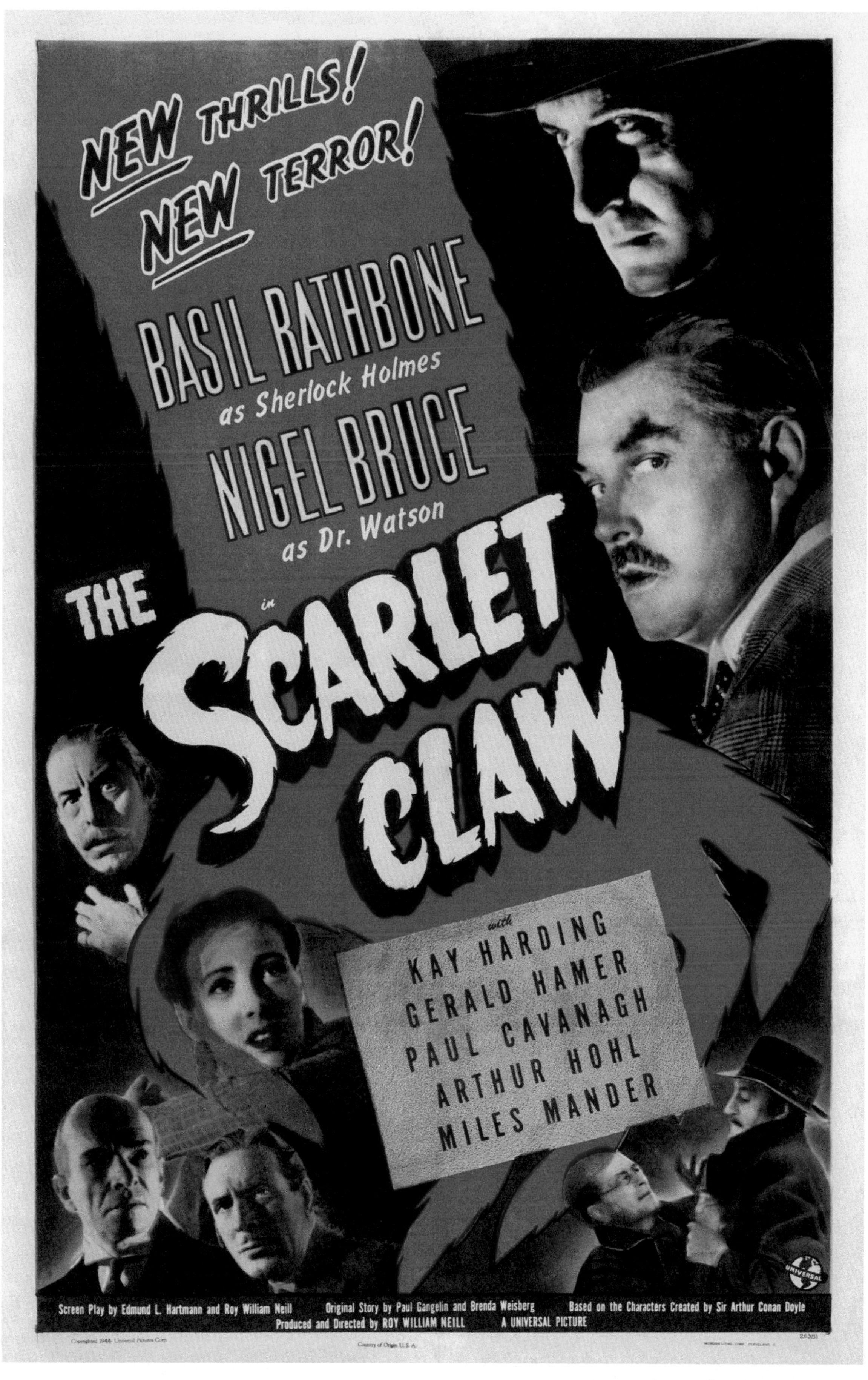

The Scarlet Claw (May 1944)
US 27 x 41 in (69 x 104 cm)

The following two pages contain US lobby cards [11 x 14 in (28 x 36 cm)] from both the original release of the film, as well as the 1948 Realart re-release.

NEW THRILLS! NEW TERROR!
BASIL RATHBONE
as Sherlock Holmes
NIGEL BRUCE
as Dr. Watson
THE SCARLET CLAW
KAY HARDING
GERALD HAMER
PAUL CAVANAGH
ARTHUR HOHL
MILES MANDER

THE SCARLET CLAW
A UNIVERSAL PICTURE

THE SCARLET CLAW
A UNIVERSAL PICTURE

THE SCARLET CLAW
A UNIVERSAL PICTURE

THE SCARLET CLAW
A UNIVERSAL PICTURE

THE SCARLET CLAW
A UNIVERSAL PICTURE

THE SCARLET CLAW
A UNIVERSAL PICTURE

THE SCARLET CLAW
A UNIVERSAL PICTURE

"THE RED-DEATH STRIKES"
BASIL RATHBONE
AS SHERLOCK HOLMES
NIGEL BRUCE
AS DR. WATSON
THE SCARLET CLAW
KAY HARDING • GERALD HAMER
PAUL CAVANAGH
ARTHUR HOHL
MILES MANDER
48/1539

BASIL RATHBONE
AS SHERLOCK HOLMES
NIGEL BRUCE
AS DR. WATSON
THE SCARLET CLAW
48/1539

BASIL RATHBONE
AS SHERLOCK HOLMES
NIGEL BRUCE
AS DR. WATSON
THE SCARLET CLAW
48/1539

BASIL RATHBONE
AS SHERLOCK HOLMES
NIGEL BRUCE
AS DR. WATSON
THE SCARLET CLAW
48/1539

BASIL RATHBONE
AS SHERLOCK HOLMES
NIGEL BRUCE
AS DR. WATSON
THE SCARLET CLAW
48/1539

BASIL RATHBONE
AS SHERLOCK HOLMES
NIGEL BRUCE
AS DR. WATSON
THE SCARLET CLAW
48/1539

BASIL RATHBONE
AS SHERLOCK HOLMES
NIGEL BRUCE
AS DR. WATSON
THE SCARLET CLAW
48/1539

BASIL RATHBONE
AS SHERLOCK HOLMES
NIGEL BRUCE
AS DR. WATSON
THE SCARLET CLAW
48/1539

The Scarlet Claw (May 1944)
Australia 13 x 30 in (33 x 84 cm)

The Scarlet Claw (May 1944)
Australia 13 x 30 in (33 x 84 cm)

The Scarlet Claw (May 1944)
US 22 x 28 in (56 x 71 cm)

The Scarlet Claw Realart Re-release: (December 1948)
US 22 x 28 in (56 x 71 cm)

The Scarlet Claw - Realart Re-Release (December 1948)
US 27 x 41 in (69 x 104 cm)

The Pearl of Death was released in the U.S. August 1, 1944. The screenplay was written by Bertram Millhauser, which was based on the Arthur Conan Doyle story *The Six Napoleons*. It was produced and directed by Roy William Neill.

The story opens at sea with the lovely Evelyn Ankers (Naomi Drake) breaking into another passenger's cabin, just as the ship is arriving at the White Cliffs of Dover. Ms. Drake enlists the help of a clergyman shipmate whom she befriended, to unwittingly smuggle her stolen goods (the Borgia Pearl) through customs. Knowing that a clergyman would be above suspicion, she felt it would be safer to have him carry the pearl past the customs agents. Once past the checkpoint, she meets up with the clergyman who returns her camera to her and she rushes off with the spoils of her crime. After meeting her accomplice, Giles Conover (Miles Mander), she hands the camera over to him to remove the pearl. The empty camera contains only a note that read "My dear Conover, forgive me if I take the liberty of returning the Borgia Pearl to its lawful owners, devotedly S.H.". Conover immediately realizes that they have been outsmarted by none other than Sherlock Holmes.

After a visit from Inspector Lestrade (Dennis Hoey), the pearl is returned to its rightful home at the Royal Regent Museum. Francis Digby (Charles Francis), the curator, demonstrates the elaborate security system in place to protect the pearl. In a post-demonstration discussion in Digby's office, Sherlock quickly demonstrates how easy it would be for someone to circumvent the security system. However an observant crook takes advantage of Sherlock's wit and escapes with the pearl. Minutes later, Conover is apprehended while running away from the museum, however, he is not in possession of the pearl.

Lestrade enters Baker St. and mentions that a Major Harker had his back broken and was killed that afternoon. The three men depart for the scene of the crime and after a short investigation Holmes reveals that the Major had been killed by "The Creeper" (Rondo Hatton), a known associate of Conover's. Along with the residence being heavily decorated with Napoleonic bric-a-brac, for reasons unknown, the body was found surrounded by broken china. As Holmes and Watson depart for home, a car drives by and shots ring out in their direction.

The following day, a visitor drops by Baker Street to leave a rare book as a thank-you gesture for Holmes' work on a family matter. Holmes arrives home to find Watson with the gift, however his intuition tells him that something is amiss, so he carefully opens the book, only to find it booby-trapped, and he narrowly misses being stabbed by a spring-loaded dagger. Later that day, they learn that another body has been found with a broken back in a litter of smashed china. In the days to follow, several similar murders occur, each body being left surrounded by broken china.

As Holmes combs through the debris from the crime scenes, he notices that each appears to have at least one thing in common…among the broken china there appears to have been a bust of Napoleon at each scene. Further investigation leads them to a small pottery shop near the museum, and they soon realize that Conover rushed into the shop when he fled with the pearl and slipped it inside of one of a group of recently cast busts of Napoleon. Each of the busts is traced back to one of the murder victims or was smashed before it left the shop. There was only one remaining bust that had been sold to a local doctor, Julien Boncourt (John Merkyl). Holmes was immediately en route to the doctor's residence, hoping to arrive before Conover. Conover enters and confronts the doctor, looking for the bust, but he is quickly surprised to find Holmes standing in for the doctor and holding him at gunpoint. Holmes has again proven to be one step ahead of the criminals.

The Pearl of Death (August 1944)
US 27 x 41 in (69 x 104 cm)

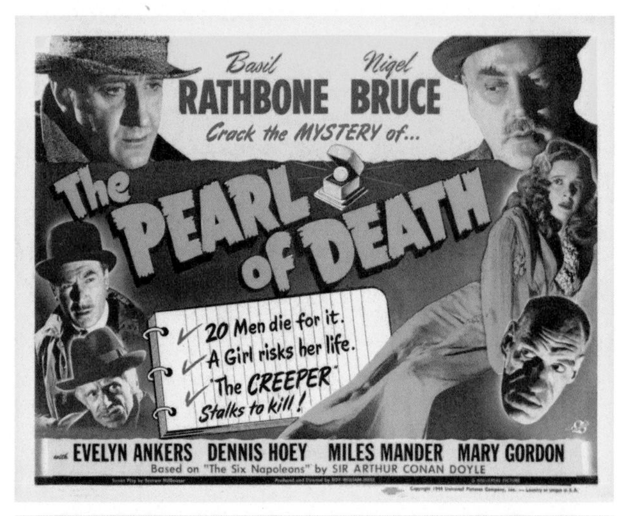
Basil
Nigel
RATHBONE BRUCE
Crack the MYSTERY of...
The PEARL of DEATH
20 Men die for it.
A Girl risks her life.
"The CREEPER" Stalks to kill!
with EVELYN ANKERS DENNIS HOEY MILES MANDER MARY GORDON
Based on "The Six Napoleons" by SIR ARTHUR CONAN DOYLE

The PEARL of DEATH
A UNIVERSAL PICTURE

The PEARL of DEATH
A UNIVERSAL PICTURE

The PEARL of DEATH
A UNIVERSAL PICTURE

The PEARL of DEATH
A UNIVERSAL PICTURE

The PEARL of DEATH
A UNIVERSAL PICTURE

The PEARL of DEATH
A UNIVERSAL PICTURE

The PEARL of DEATH
A UNIVERSAL PICTURE

The Pearl of Death (August 1944)
Sweden 27½ x 39½ in (70 x 100 cm)

Left:
The Pearl of Death (August 1944)
US 11 x 14 in (28 x 36 cm)

Sherlock Holmes - The House of Fear was released on March 16, 1945 and was based on the Conan Doyle story *The Adventure of the Five Orange Pips*. This installment was produced and directed by Roy William Neill.

The story opens with the seven members of the "Good Comrades" club seated for dinner and their housekeeper, Mrs. Montieth (Sally Shepherd), delivering a telegram to club member Ralph King (Richard Alexander). Mr. King and his comrades laugh at the letter, thinking it a joke; although Mrs. Monteith knows better. The following day, King dies horribly in a car crash.

One by one, club members are killed in gruesome fashion, their bodies left unrecognizable.

Holmes and Watson head off to the club members' mansion in Scotland, after being engaged by an insurance underwriter, Mr. Chalmers, (played by Gavin Muir), who feels there has been foul play that has his company paying out on policies to the surviving club members.

Things start to fall in place when a local business owner, Alex MacGregor, (played by David Clyde) is murdered after sending Inspector Lestrade (Dennis Hoey) a note telling them that he doesn't believe in ghosts. Holmes surmises that if he talking about ghosts, he must have seen one.

When we get down to one remaining club member, Bruce Alastair, (played by Aubrey Mather), Lestrade takes him into custody assuming he is the killer. Watson stumbles across the fact that Captain John Simpson's (Harry Cording) prized pipe tobacco is missing from its holder and Holmes has the final piece of the puzzle he needs to solve the mystery. He finds a secret passageway down to the basement, where the club members are found alive and well with insurance money in hand!

The House of Fear (March 1945)
US 22 x 28 in (56 x 71 cm)

The House of Fear (March 1945)
US 27 x 41 in (69 x 104 cm)

HORROR Stalking its Halls!
The HOUSE of FEAR
starring Basil RATHBONE Nigel BRUCE
with
AUBREY MATHER GAVIN MUIR DENNIS HOEY PAUL CAVANAGH HOLMES HERBERT
Based on "The Adventure of the Five Orange Pips" by SIR ARTHUR CONAN DOYLE

THE HOUSE of FEAR
A UNIVERSAL PICTURE
44/380

THE HOUSE of FEAR
A UNIVERSAL PICTURE
44/380

THE HOUSE of FEAR
A UNIVERSAL PICTURE
44/380

THE HOUSE of FEAR
A UNIVERSAL PICTURE
44/380

THE HOUSE of FEAR
A UNIVERSAL PICTURE
44/380

THE HOUSE of FEAR
A UNIVERSAL PICTURE
44/380

THE HOUSE of FEAR
A UNIVERSAL PICTURE
44/380

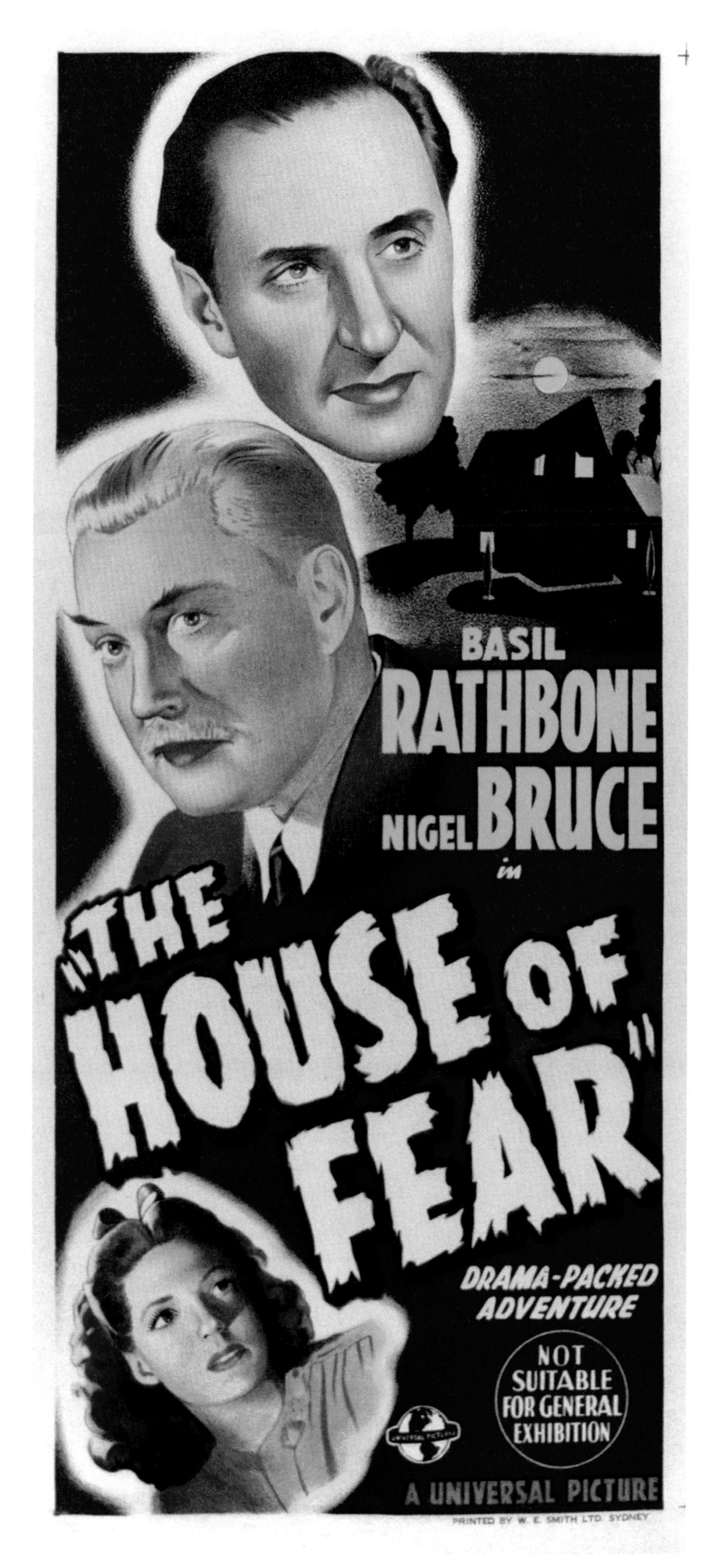

The House of Fear (March 1945)
Australia 13 x 30 in (33 x 84 cm)

Left:
The House of Fear (March 1945)
US 11 x 14 in (28 x 36 cm)

The House of Fear (March 1945)
Sweden 27½ x 39½ in (70 x 100 cm)

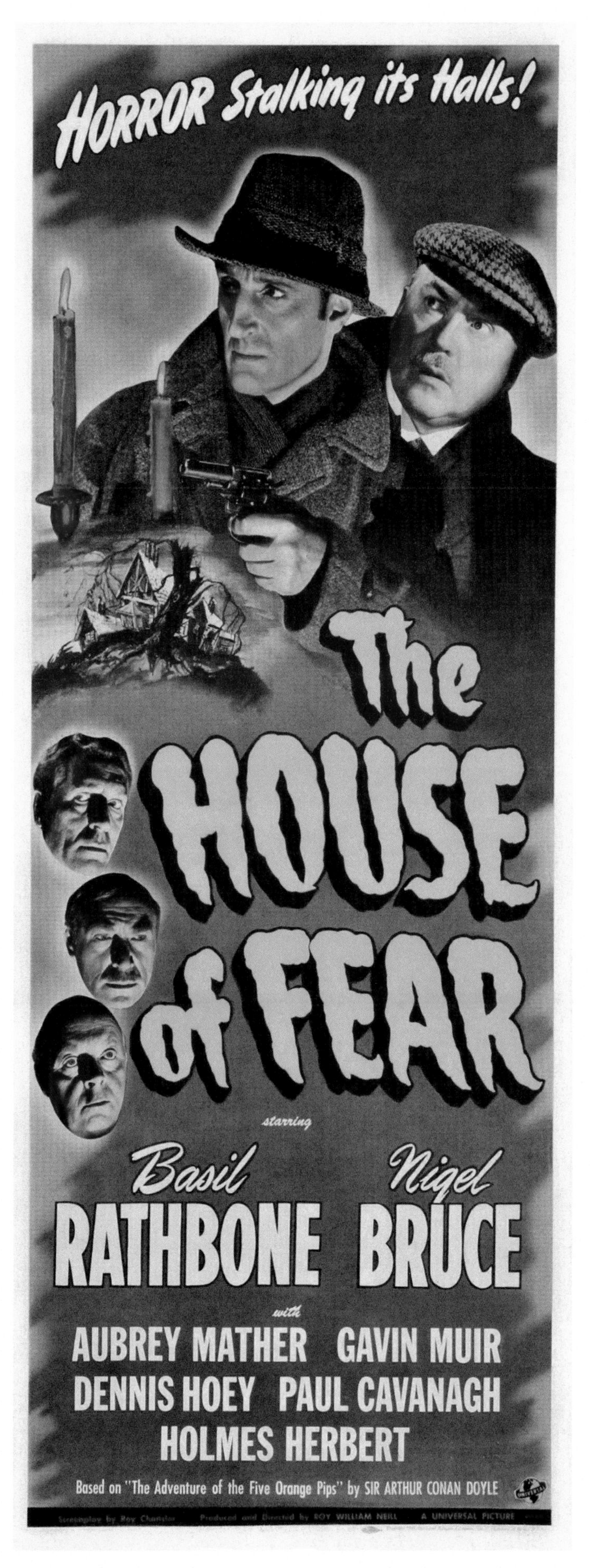

The House of Fear (March 1945)
US 14 x 36 in (36 x 91 cm)

The Woman in Green released on July 27, 1945, was based on Conan Doyle's *The Adventure of the Empty House*, with an original screenplay by Bertram Millhauser.

With four women brutally murdered in London, Inspector Gregson (Matthew Boulton) of the London police calls on the help of Sherlock Holmes. The killer murders his victims and then almost surgically cuts off a finger as somewhat of a trophy.

Lydia Marlowe (Hillary Brooke), a young socialite, is involved with Sir George Fenwick, (played by Paul Cavanagh) who is several years her senior. After a nightcap at Marlowe's apartment, Sir George wakes up dazed and confused in a low-rent hotel room, with apparently no memory of how he got there. Through the hotel window, Sir George hears a newspaper boy announcing that there has been another brutal murder. He quickly tries to retrace his footsteps by returning to Lydia's flat, looking for answers. While explaining his dilemma to her, there is a knock at the door, from a man wanting to speak with Sir George. The stranger produces an engraved silver case which bears the initials of Sir George. When asked where he obtained the case, the stranger tells a story of seeing it fall out of Sir George's pocket, while he was bending over something with a knife in his hand.

After Sir George is found dead, Holmes starts to puzzle the situation together, coming to the conclusion that his death was connected to an elaborate blackmail scheme masterminded by none other than Professor Moriarty.

With a hypnotized Holmes just footsteps from death, Watson and the police arrive just in time to save the day, as Holmes had planned all along.

The Woman in Green (July 1945)
US 22 x 28 in (56 x 71 cm)

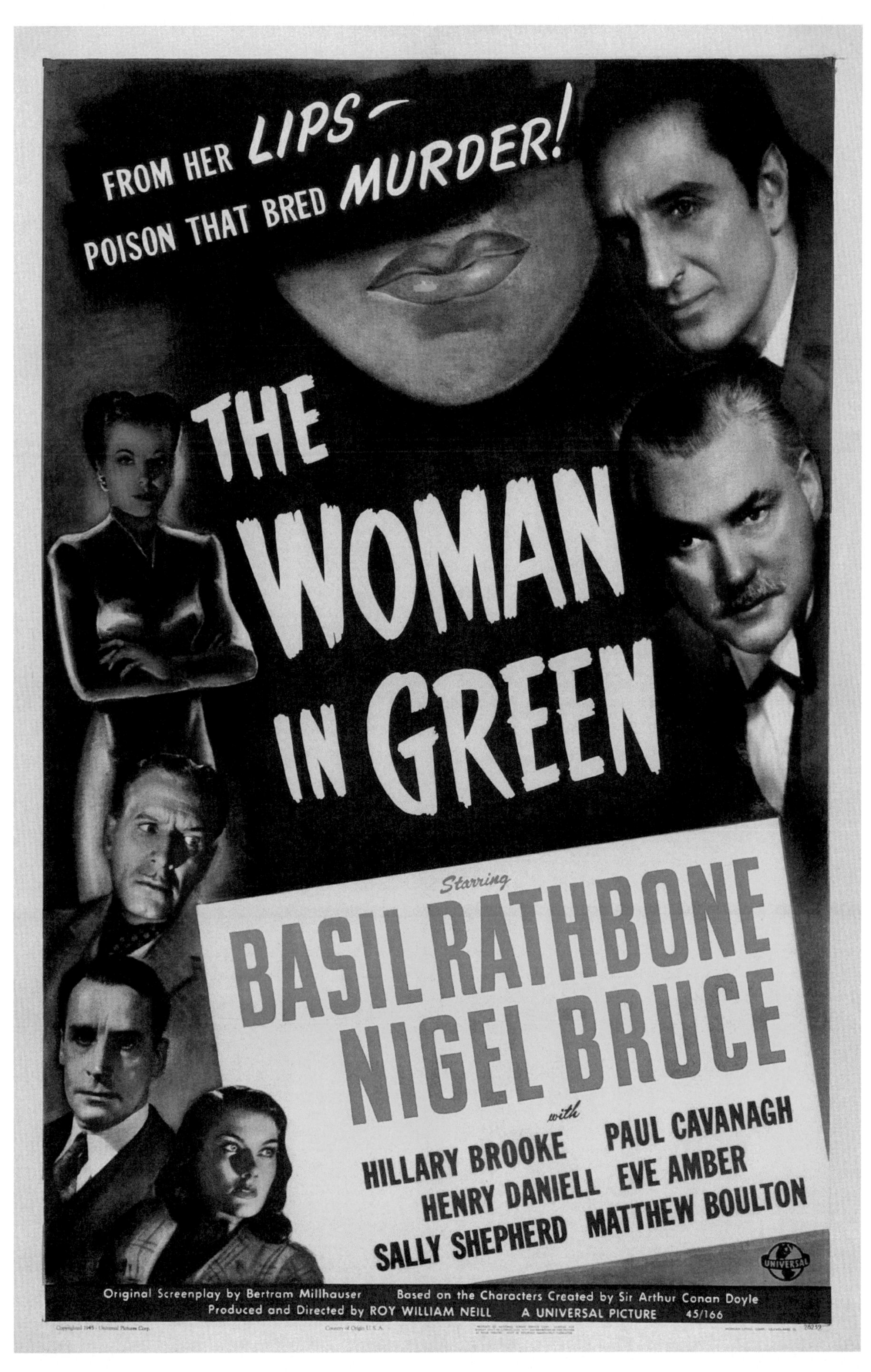

The Woman in Green (July 1945)
US 27 x 41 in (69 x 104 cm)

TEMPTRESS OF PLEASURE
OR MISTRESS OF MURDER?
THE WOMAN
IN GREEN
Starring
BASIL RATHBONE
NIGEL BRUCE
with
HILLARY BROOKE
PAUL CAVANAGH
HENRY DANIELL
EVE AMBER
SALLY SHEPHERD
MATTHEW BOULTON

THE
WOMAN
IN GREEN
A UNIVERSAL PICTURE
45/166

THE
WOMAN
IN GREEN
A UNIVERSAL PICTURE
45/166

THE
WOMAN
IN GREEN
A UNIVERSAL PICTURE
45/166

THE
WOMAN
IN GREEN
A UNIVERSAL PICTURE
45/166

THE
WOMAN
IN GREEN
A UNIVERSAL PICTURE
45/166

THE
WOMAN
IN GREEN
A UNIVERSAL PICTURE
45/166

THE
WOMAN
IN GREEN
A UNIVERSAL PICTURE
45/166

The Woman in Green (July 1945)
Sweden 27½ x 39½ in (70 x 100 cm)

Left:
The Woman in Green (July 1945)
US 11 x 14 in (28 x 36 cm)

The Woman in Green (July 1945)
US 14 x 36 in (36 x 91 cm)

The Woman in Green (July 1945)
US 81 x 81 in (206 x 206 cm)

Pursuit to Algiers was released in the U.S. on October 26, 1945. The film was based on an original screenplay by Leonard Lee and produced and directed by Roy William Neill.

The story opens with Holmes and Watson being lured into a fish and chip shop to receive a coded message sending them to a residence in Fishbone Alley. Holmes soon finds that a group representing the government of Rovina is soliciting his assistance in getting the son of their recently assassinated king safely back to their country. To Watson's dismay, Holmes accepts the mission in the name of democracy everywhere.

We soon discover that Holmes is to fly with the prince back to Rovina, but due to a suspiciously timed "accident," the replacement plane they will be taking has only room for two passengers, leaving no room for Watson. Holmes is immediately suspicious, rightfully so, and directs Watson to conspicuously travel to the Mediterranean by sea, where they will ultimately reunite.

The Swedish ship SS Friesland sets sail (with Watson onboard) for Alexandria. Early in the voyage, Watson sees a Wireless News Bulletin posted on the ship which reports that a small three-seat plane crashed over Pyrenees, with all occupants feared lost. Shortly thereafter, a purser approaches Watson requesting his help with an ill passenger. Despite being distraught over the presumed death of Holmes on the downed flight, Watson agrees to help. When he visits the passenger's cabin, he finds the room occupied by Sherlock himself, accompanied by the young prince. The three agree that Nikolas will be introduced as Watson's nephew to help establish a cover for him.

The passengers notice the ship's engines shutting down, and the ship comes to a standstill unexpectedly, just off the coast of Lisbon. Holmes surmises that they will soon be joined by a few new passengers, who may have learned that he and Nikolas were not aboard the downed flight. Not coincidentally, the new passengers -- Mirco (Martin Kosleck), Gregor (Rex Evan), and Gubec (William 'Wee Willie' Davis) -- take up residence in the room across from Holmes. The next morning, Nikolas is nearly poisoned with a cyanide laced cup of coffee, which Watson suggests as possibly being the work of their suspicious steward Sanford (Morton Lowry). Another failed attempt on Nikolas' life occurs at dinner on the final night of the voyage, as Holmes identifies a "party favor" that is, in fact, a bomb left to explode when Nikolas handles it. It appears that Holmes and Watson will finally be able to complete their mission and deliver the new king safely to Algiers, as the ship comes to a stop just off the coast of their destination. Watson takes a launch ashore to pick up the government's representatives, leaving Holmes and Nikolas to await their return. Moments later, a knock at the door claims to be Watson; however, as Nikolas answers, Gregor, Mirco and Gubec enter with guns drawn. Holmes is tied up and knocked out, while Nikolas is escorted away.

Watson and the Prince's entourage return to escort him home, only to find Nikolas missing and Holmes restrained. His countrymen are gravely concerned when it appears that their King has been lost. Holmes instructs Watson to summon the steward to their room. As Sanford arrives, Holmes introduces him as the King to an astonished Watson. In true Holmsian style, the Prince has been hiding in plain sight, and Nikolas (who was safely rescued) was there to throw the crooks off track.

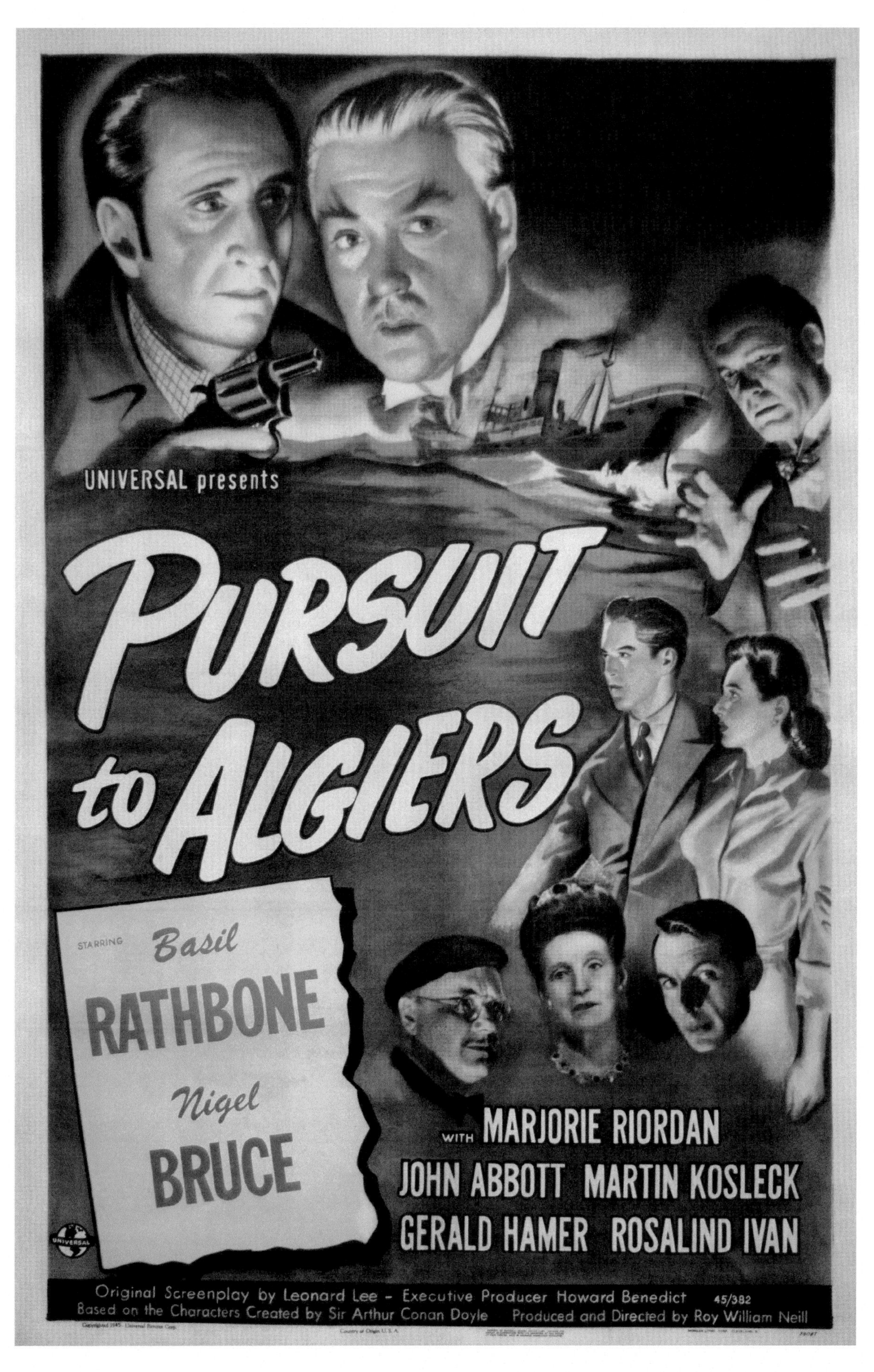

Pursuit to Algiers (October 1945)
US 27 x 41 in (69 x 104 cm)

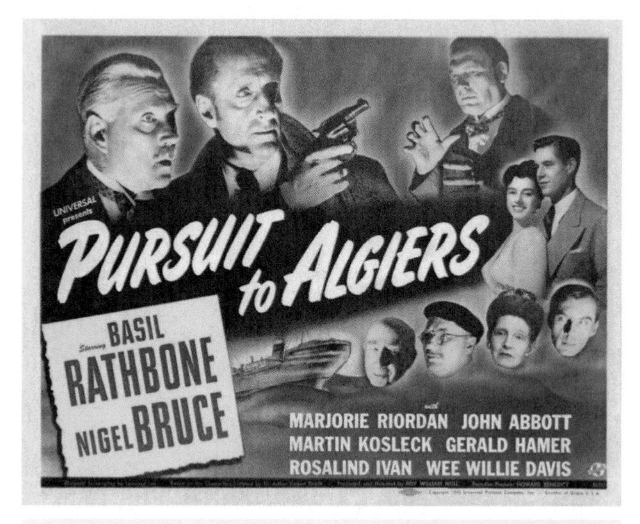
UNIVERSAL presents
PURSUIT to ALGIERS
Starring BASIL RATHBONE
NIGEL BRUCE
with
MARJORIE RIORDAN JOHN ABBOTT
MARTIN KOSLECK GERALD HAMER
ROSALIND IVAN WEE WILLIE DAVIS

PURSUIT to ALGIERS
A UNIVERSAL PICTURE

PURSUIT to ALGIERS
A UNIVERSAL PICTURE

PURSUIT to ALGIERS
A UNIVERSAL PICTURE

PURSUIT to ALGIERS
A UNIVERSAL PICTURE

PURSUIT to ALGIERS
A UNIVERSAL PICTURE

PURSUIT to ALGIERS
A UNIVERSAL PICTURE

PURSUIT to ALGIERS
A UNIVERSAL PICTURE

Pursuit to Algiers (October 1945)
Sweden 27½ x 39½ in (70 x 100 cm)

Left:
Pursuit to Algiers (October 1945)
US 11 x 14 in (28 x 36 cm)

Pursuit to Algiers (October 1945)
US 41" x 81" (104 x 206 cm)

*This poster was printed in the United States for use at theaters with Spanish speaking audiences.

Pursuit to Algiers (October 1945)
US* 27 x 41 in (69 x 104 cm)

Terror by Night was released in the U.S. on February 1, 1946, featuring an original screenplay by Frank Gruber, although it does draw elements from several of Conan Doyle's stories, including *The Sign of Four* and *The Adventures of the Empty House.*

The story opens with a brief history lesson on "one of the most famous of the earth's treasures" -- the "Star of Rhodesia" -- a 453 carat diamond with a notorious history of leading its owners to violent deaths.

After being hired by Roland Carstairs (Geoffrey Steele), Holmes and Watson are on the job, protecting his mother, Lady Margaret's (played by Mary Forbes) prized Star of Rhodesia, on a London to Edinburgh train tour. Fellow passengers include Vivian Vedder (Renee Godfrey), who is transporting her mother's body to Scotland for burial, Maj. Duncan-Bleek (Alan Mowbray), a longtime friend of Watson and Inspector Lestrade (Dennis Hoey) of Scotland Yard.

After Roland is murdered and the diamond stolen, everyone on the train becomes a suspect. As the investigation unfolds, Holmes surmises that this is a case where things are not always as they seem and there must be another party involved...but where could the culprit be hiding?

The extra-large casket seems suspicious to Holmes and he quickly discovers an empty hidden compartment, large enough to conceal a second person.

Sometimes people are not what they seem either, and we quickly learn that Watson's friend is, in fact, a notorious criminal who is working with the casket stowaway to steal the diamond.

As usual, Holmes is a step ahead of the criminals, having earlier switched out the "Star of Rhodesia" with a fake, so in reality the real diamond was safe and sound all along and ultimately the bad guys end up in handcuffs.

Terror by Night (February 1946)
US 22 x 28 in (56 x 71 cm)

Terror by Night (February 1946)
US 27 x 41 in (69 x 104 cm)

UNIVERSAL PRESENTS
TERROR BY NIGHT
Starring
Basil RATHBONE
Nigel BRUCE
ALAN MOWBRAY
RENEE GODFREY
DENNIS HOEY
BILLY BEVAN

TERROR BY NIGHT
A UNIVERSAL PICTURE
46/502

TERROR BY NIGHT
A UNIVERSAL PICTURE
46/502

TERROR BY NIGHT
A UNIVERSAL PICTURE
46/502

TERROR BY NIGHT
A UNIVERSAL PICTURE
46/502

TERROR BY NIGHT
A UNIVERSAL PICTURE
46/502

TERROR BY NIGHT
A UNIVERSAL PICTURE
46/502

TERROR BY NIGHT
A UNIVERSAL PICTURE
46/502

Left:
Terror by Night (February 1946)
US 11 x 14 in (28 x 36 cm)

Terror by Night (February 1946)
US 41" x 81" (104 x 206 cm)

Terror by Night (February 1946)
US 14 x 36 in (36 x 91 cm)

Terror by Night (February 1946)
Sweden 27½ x 39½ in (70 x 100 cm)

Dressed to Kill was released in the U.S. on June 7, 1946. Despite being based on Arthur Conan Doyle's characters, *Dressed to Kill* (originally titled *Prelude to Murder*) is an original story by writer Frank Gruber, which was later re-worked by screenwriter Leonard Lee. This was the fourteenth and final Sherlock Holmes film in which Basil Rathbone and Nigel Bruce starred together.

Dartmoor Prison resident, John Davidson, crafts three small music boxes which make their way to the Gaylord Gallery to be auctioned. The rather plain boxes are each sold to different parties, setting up a soon to be scavenger hunt. After the auction, the gallery director, Ebenezer Crabtree (Holmes Herbert), is bribed to provide the purchasers' identities by a well-dressed stranger, Colonel Cavanaugh (played by Frederick Worlock), who himself had planned on purchasing the three boxes.

After the owner of the first music box, Julian 'Stinky' Emery (Edmund Breon), is murdered, Holmes is quickly on the case to discover the identity of the perpetrator. The owner of the second box, a young girl (Topsy Glyn) got off more easily, having been tied up, gagged and placed in a closet. When the crooks, Mrs. Hilda Courtney (Patricia Morison), Colonel Cavanaugh, and Hamid (Harry Cording) attempt to acquire the third box, they learn that Sherlock Holmes himself is the new owner.

Holmes takes the box to Scotland Yard in an attempt to discover the hidden mystery, which has left at least one man dead. X-raying the box provides no clue to its secrets; however, Holmes becomes curious about the melody played by the box. Scotland Yard determines that music boxes were all made by the same inmate...one John Davidson...a man in prison for stealing British 5-pound printing plates from the Bank of England. The plates were never recovered, despite Davidson being arrested just fifteen minutes after the theft. With this information in hand, Holmes and the police determine that this crime revolves around the stolen printing plates.

Working with musician friend, Joe Cisto (Wallace Scott), Holmes starts to suspect a hidden code within the melody on the three boxes. After a somewhat off the cuff remark by Watson the following morning, Holmes surmises that the note variations in the melody correspond to piano keys and specific letters in the alphabet. Things are now much clearer and the hunt is on for the meaning and location of the cryptic message within the tune.

Holmes gets himself into a tough situation after confronting Mrs. Hilda Courtney, who eventually makes her way to Baker Street to locate the third music box. After tricking Watson into believing there is a fire in the room, Courtney finds the location of the box and is quickly on her way to the Bank of England and her ultimate prize of the printing plates.

Holmes, Watson and Scotland Yard are hot on the heels of the crooks and wrap up the mystery when they meet a surprised Courtney and friends as they are pulling the plates from their hiding place.

Dressed to Kill (June 1946)
US 27 x 41 in (69 x 104 cm)

QUEEN...of a Crime Cult!
UNIVERSAL PRESENTS
Basil RATHBONE
Nigel BRUCE
DRESSED TO KILL
PATRICIA MORISON
EDMOND BREON FREDERIC WORLOCK
HARRY CORDING MARY GORDON

BASIL RATHBONE
NIGEL BRUCE
DRESSED TO KILL
A UNIVERSAL PICTURE

BASIL RATHBONE
NIGEL BRUCE
DRESSED TO KILL
A UNIVERSAL PICTURE

BASIL RATHBONE
NIGEL BRUCE
DRESSED TO KILL
A UNIVERSAL PICTURE

BASIL RATHBONE
NIGEL BRUCE
DRESSED TO KILL
A UNIVERSAL PICTURE

BASIL RATHBONE
NIGEL BRUCE
DRESSED TO KILL
A UNIVERSAL PICTURE

BASIL RATHBONE
NIGEL BRUCE
DRESSED TO KILL
A UNIVERSAL PICTURE

BASIL RATHBONE
NIGEL BRUCE
DRESSED TO KILL
A UNIVERSAL PICTURE

Dressed to Kill (June 1946)
US 14 x 36 in (36 x 91 cm)

Left:
Dressed to Kill (June 1946)
US 11 x 14 in (28 x 36 cm)

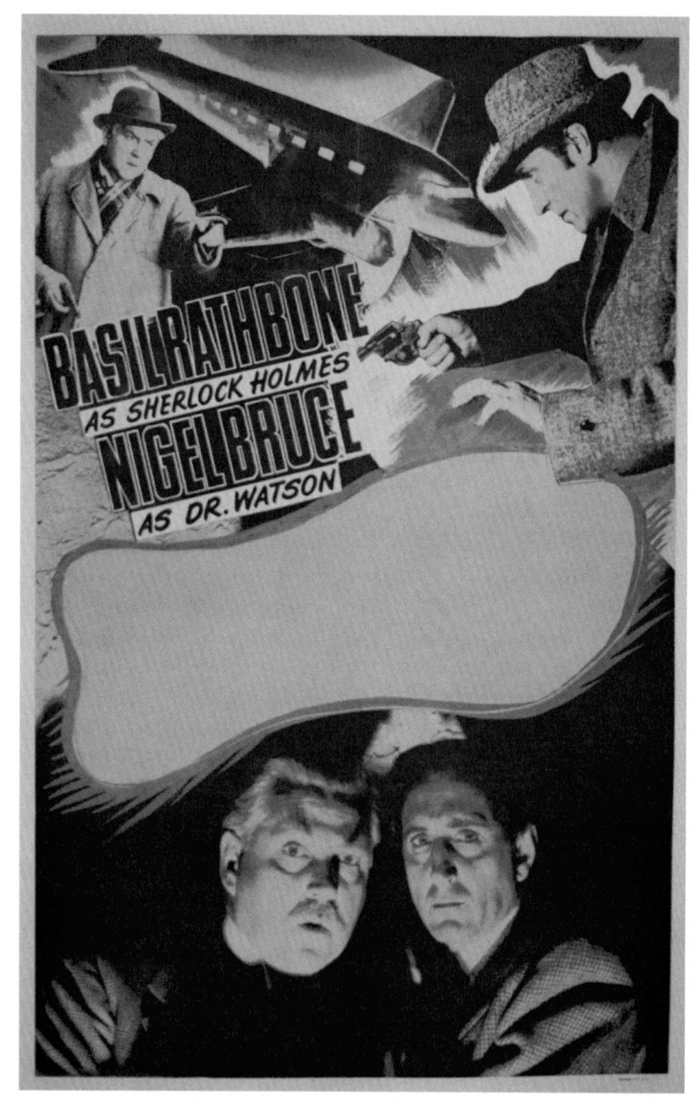

"Stock" One Sheet Poster
Printed for theatre use for re-releases of the Rathbone/ Bruce Sherlock Holmes feature films (c1950's)
US 27 x 41 in (69 x 104 cm)

Basil Rathbone finished his run as Sherlock with *Dressed to Kill* (1946), although he did reprise the role two more times in television appearances in 1953 on the series *Suspense*, and a year later as part of the *Texaco Star Theatre*.

For the next few years, there were a few appearances of Holmes, or Holmesian-like characters, in films including *The Brute Man* (1946), *My Favorite Brunette* (1947), *Merton of the Movies* (1947), *Arsenio Lupin* (1947), *Abbott and Costello Meet the Invisible Man* (1951), *Private Eyes* (1953), and *Who Done It?* (1956) with comedic actor Benny Hill in his first movie role, playing "Hugo Dill", a sweeper turned private detective.

Not until the 1956 French film *a la Maniere de Sherlock Holmes* (*In the Manner of Sherlock Holmes*) did audiences see a Sherlock feature film again. Just three years later, Holmes and Watson appeared in the 1959 Hammer Studios feature *The Hound of the Baskervilles* with Peter Cushing in the lead role. Shot in TechniColor, a key milestone was reached, allowing fans to see that everything wasn't just black and white with Sherlock Holmes. Cushing was backed up by André Morell as Watson and Christopher Lee portrayed "Sir Henry". Four years after getting his feet wet in the Arthur Conan Doyle world, Christopher Lee filled the title role in 1962's *Sherlock Holmes and the Deadly Necklace*.

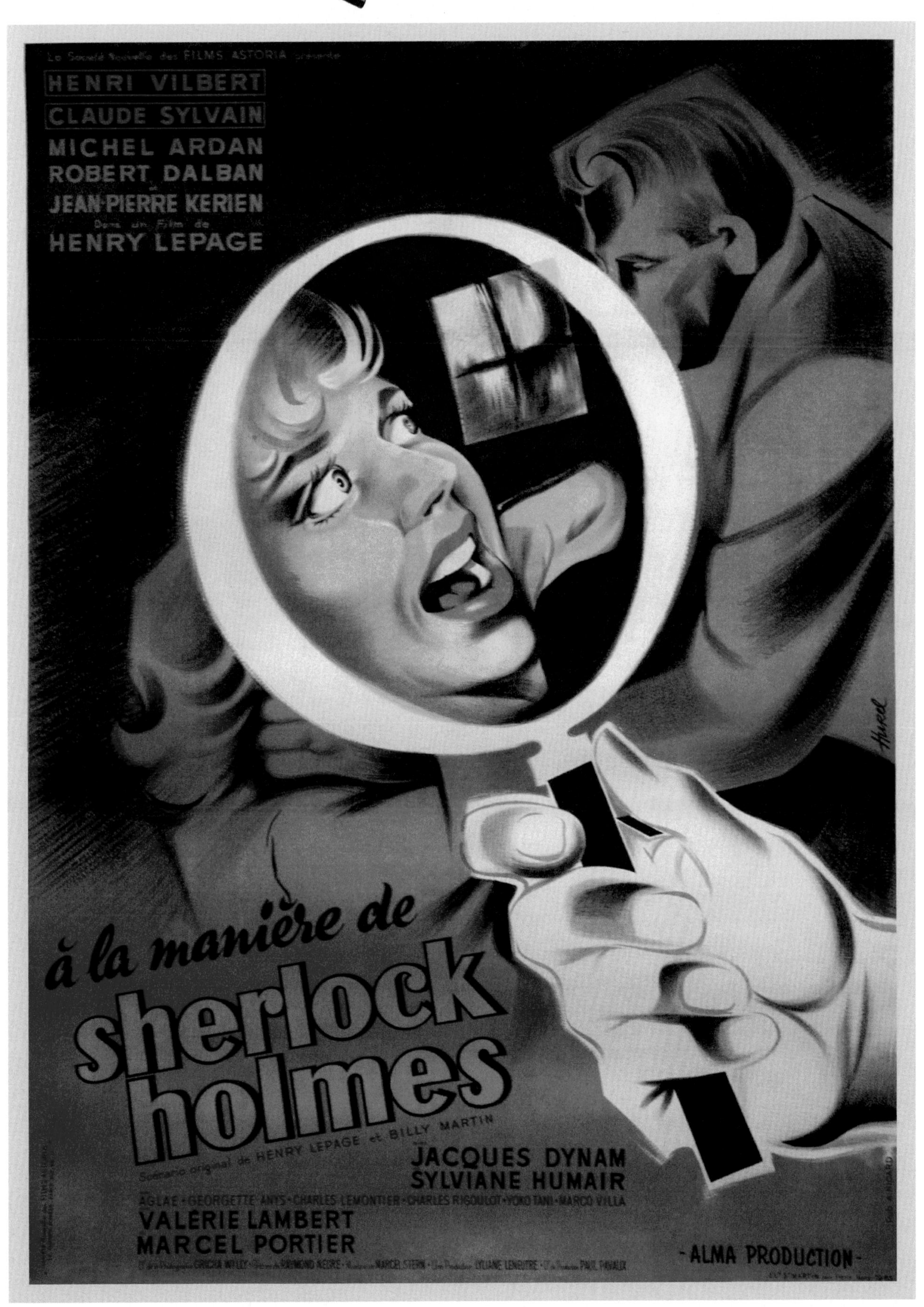

a la Maniere de Sherlock Holmes (1956)
France 47 x 63 in (119 x 160 cm)

The Brute Man (October 1946)
US 27 x 41 in (69 x 104 cm)

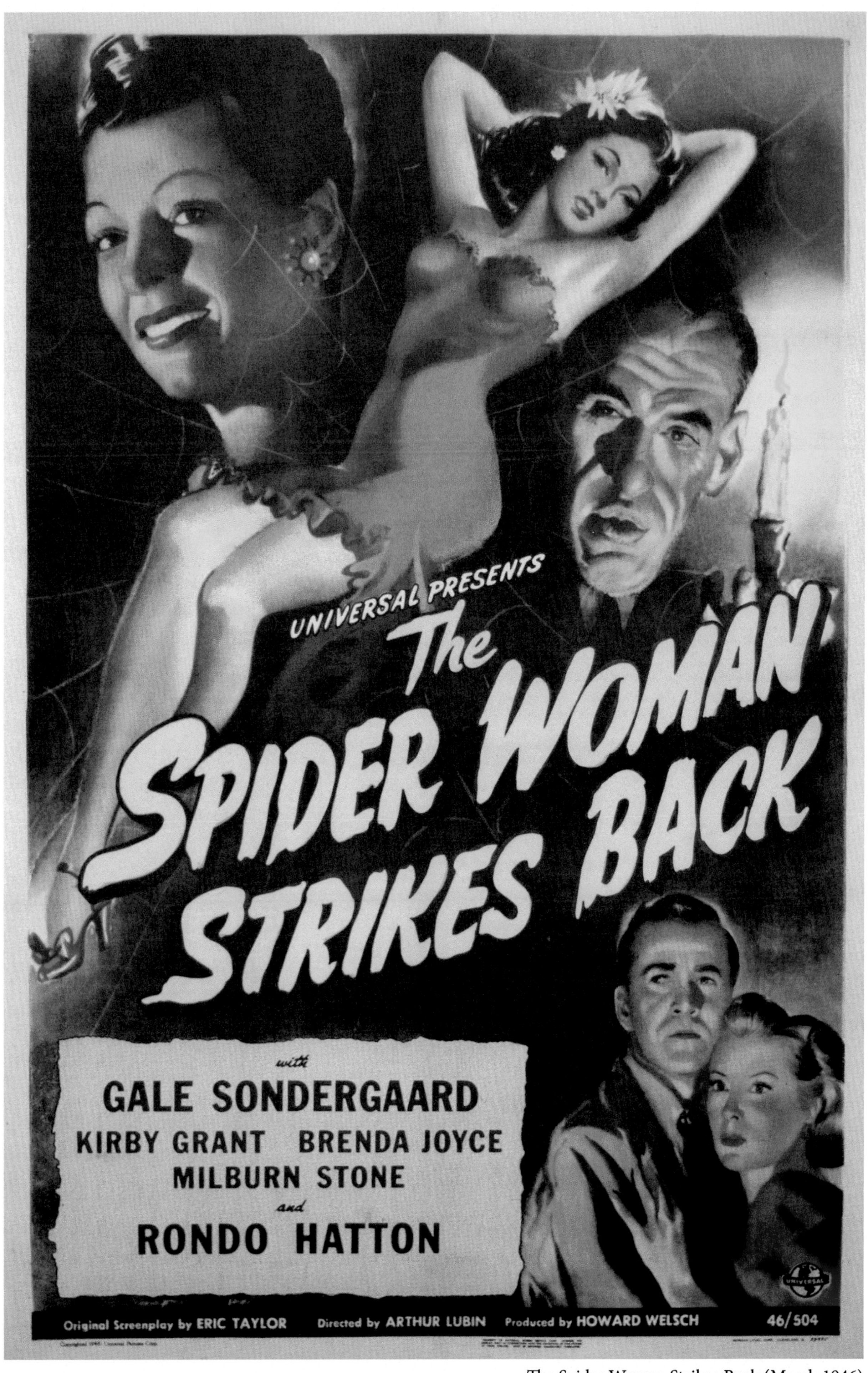

*The film is a pseudo-sequel to 1944's "The Spider Woman"

The Spider Woman Strikes Back (March 1946)
US 27 x 41 in (69 x 104 cm)

My Favorite Brunette (April 1947)
US 11 x 14 in (28 x 36 cm)

Merton of the Movies (October 1947)
US 11 x 14 in (28 x 36 cm)

Abbott and Costello Meet the Invisible Man (March 1951)
US 11 x 14 in (28 x 36 cm)

Private Eyes (December 1953)
US 11 x 14 in (28 x 36 cm)

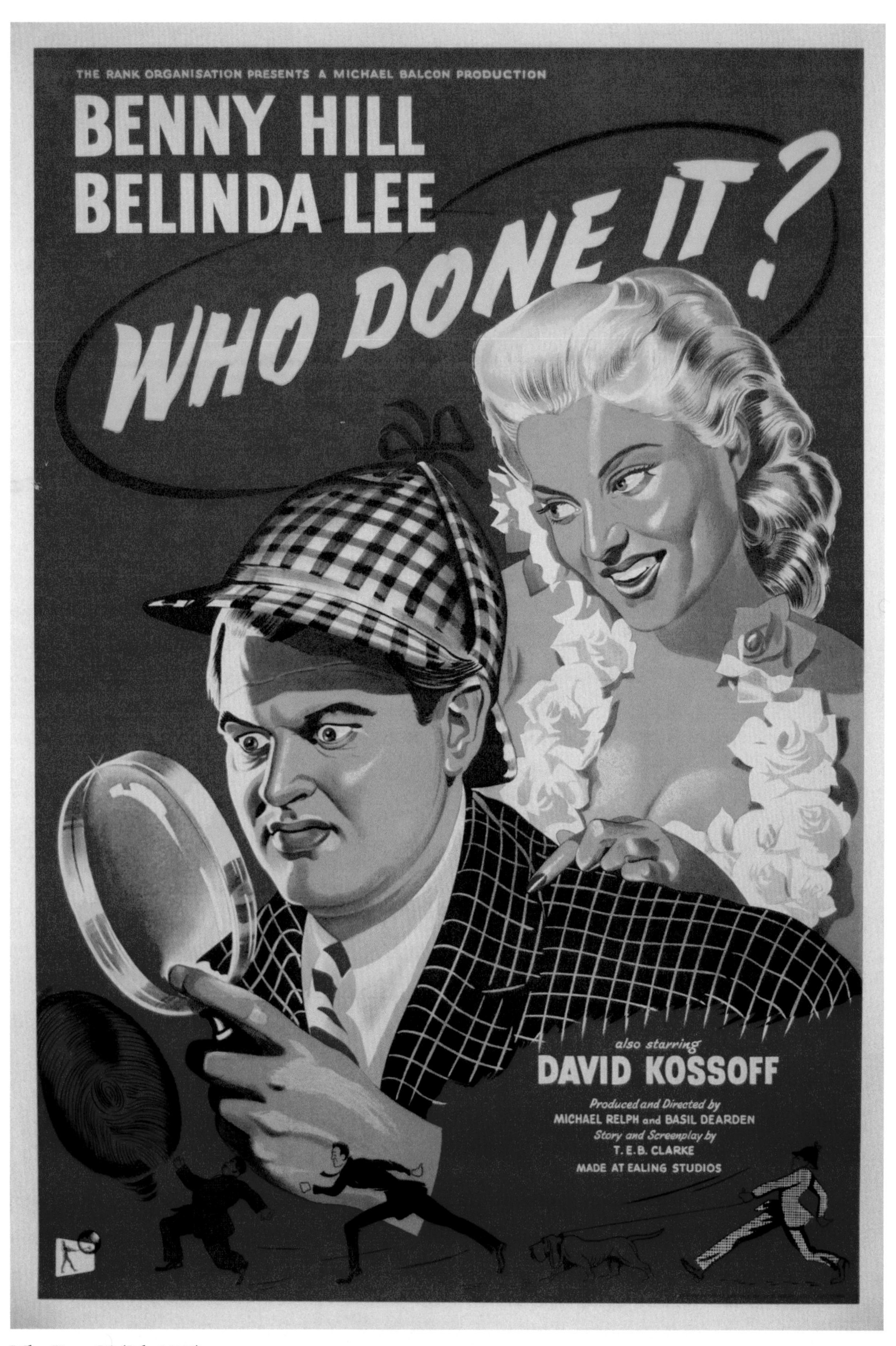

Who Done It? (July 1956)
England 27 x 39.5 in (69 x 100 cm)

It's Only Money (November 1962)
France 55 x 78 in (140 x 198 cm)

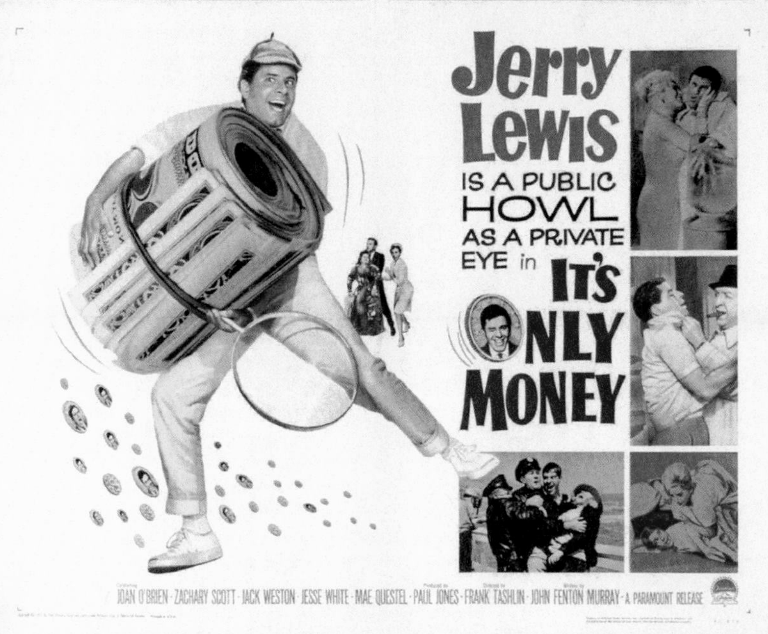

It's Only Money (November 1962)
US 22 x 28 in (56 x 71 cm)

The Hound of The Baskervilles (July 1959)
US 41 x 81 in (104 x 206 cm)

The Hound of The Baskervilles (July 1959)
Denmark 24.5 x 33.5 in (62 x 85 cm)

The Hound of The Baskervilles (July 1959)
Germany 23 x 33 in (58 x 84 cm) [1960's Re-Release]

A SIGHT TO SHATTER THE NERVES! A STORY TO STUN THE SENSES!
Never Has The Night Known A Beast Like This!
The Hound of the Baskervilles
BASED ON THE NOVEL BY SIR ARTHUR CONAN DOYLE
IT'S THE PICTURE ABOUT THAT BONE-CHILLING HOWL!
PETER CUSHING · ANDRE MORELL · CHRISTOPHER LEE
It's Ten Times The Terror in TECHNICOLOR!

The Hound of the Baskervilles

The Hound of the Baskervilles

The Hound of the Baskervilles

The Hound of the Baskervilles

The Hound of the Baskervilles

The Hound of the Baskervilles

The Hound of the Baskervilles

The Hound of The Baskervilles (July 1959)
England "Front of House" 8 x 10 in (20 x 25 cm)

Left:
The Hound of The Baskervilles (July 1959)
US 11 x 14 in (28 x 36 cm)

The Hound of The Baskervilles (July 1959)
US 27 x 41 in (69 x 104 cm)

The Hound of The Baskervilles (July 1959)
US 14 x 36 in (36 x 91 cm)

The Hound of The Baskervilles (July 1959)
US 22 x 28 in (56 x 71 cm)

The Hound of The Baskervilles (July 1959)
US 22 x 28 in (56 x 71 cm)

Sherlock Holmes and the Deadly Necklace (May 1963)
German 23 x 33 in (58 x 84 cm)

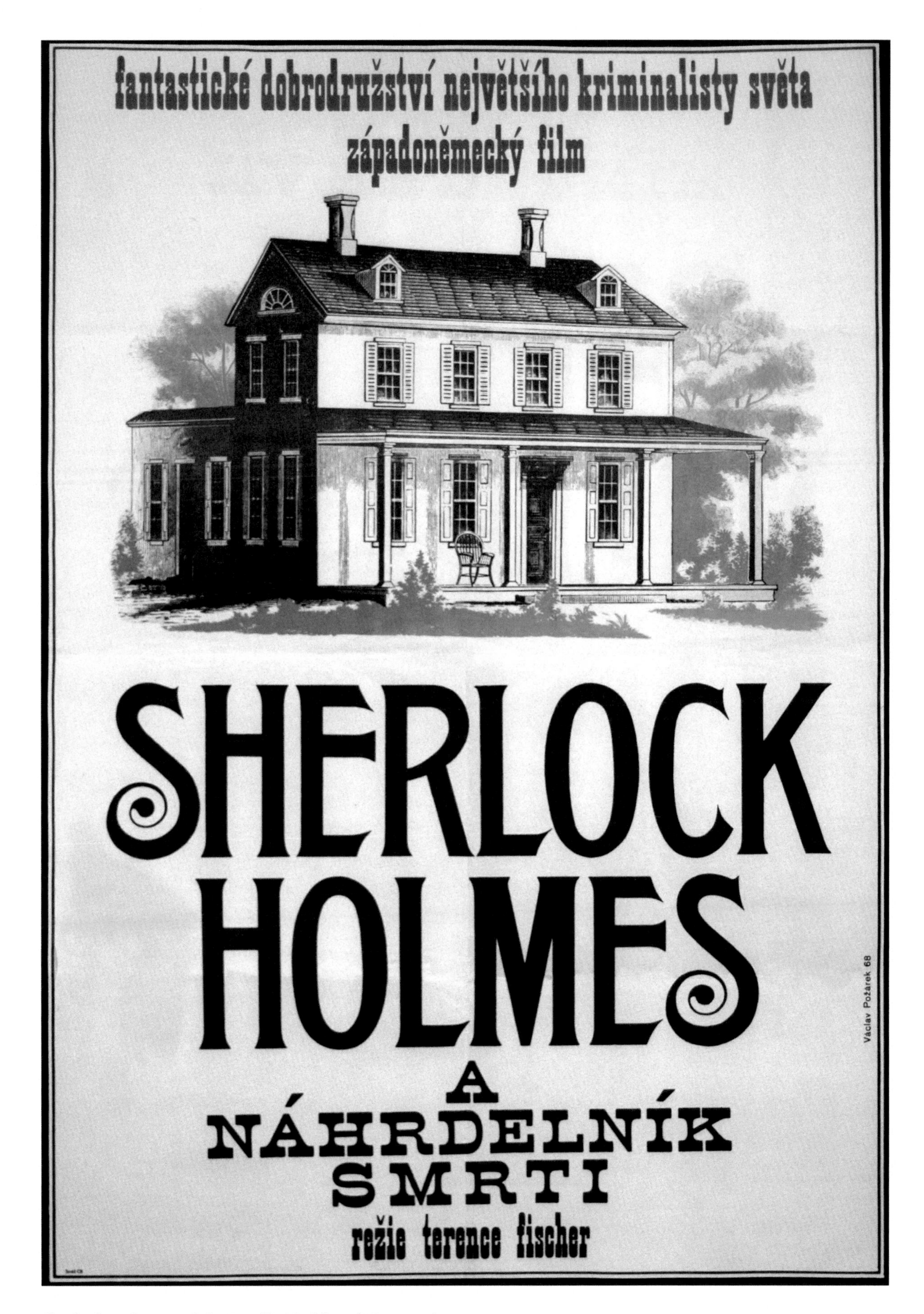

Sherlock Holmes and the Deadly Necklace (May 1963)
Czechoslovakia 23 x 33 in (58 x 84 cm)

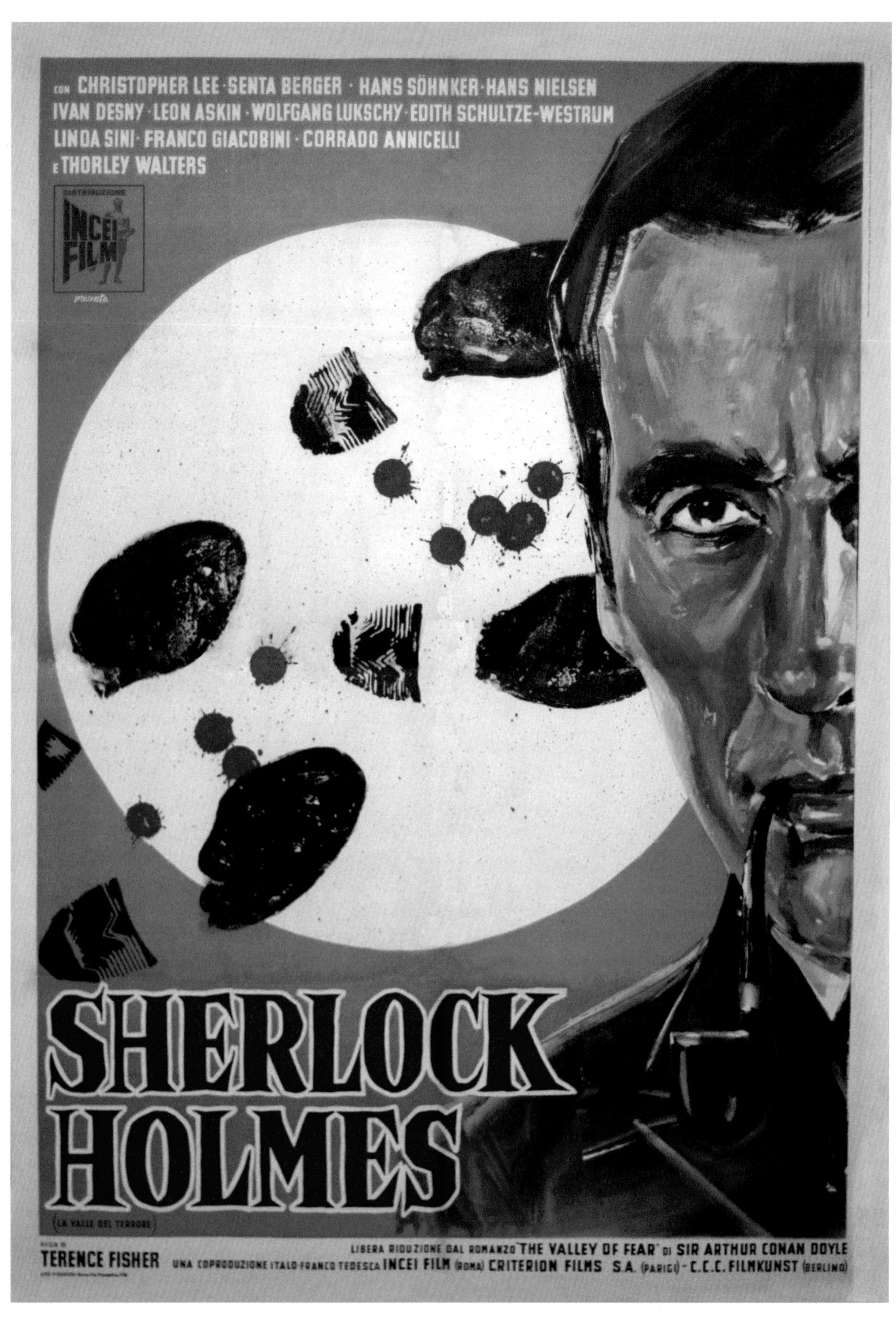

Sherlock Holmes and the Deadly Necklace (May 1963)
Italy 39 x 55 in (99 x 140 cm)

A Study in Terror (August 1966)
German 23 x 33 in (58 x 84 cm)

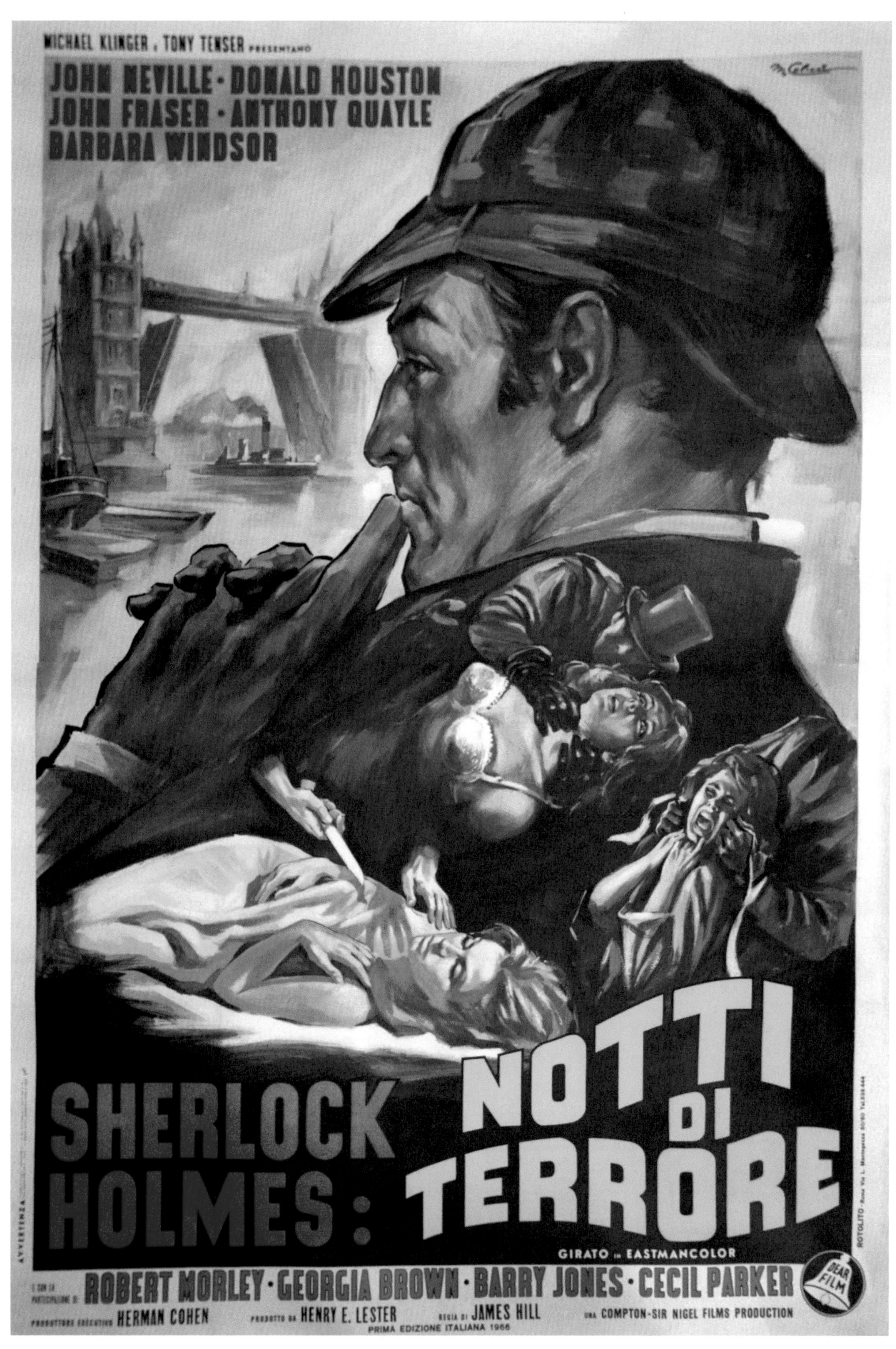

A Study in Terror (August 1966)
Italy 55 x 78 in (140 x 198 cm)

A Study in Terror (August 1966)
France 23 x 31 in (60 x 80 cm)

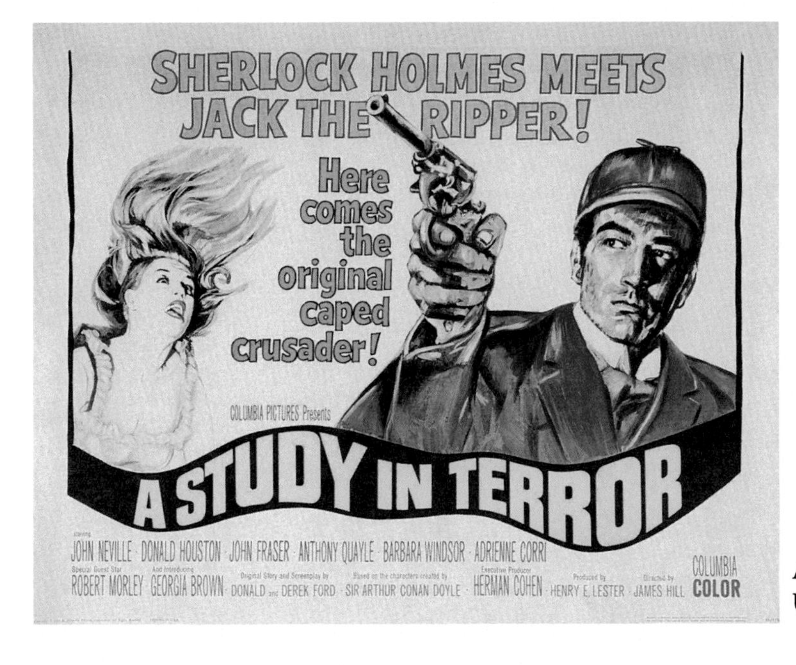

A Study in Terror (August 1966)
US 22 x 28 in (56 x 71 cm)

The Private Life of Sherlock Holmes (October 1970)
France 47 x 63 in (119 x 160 cm)

The Private Life of Sherlock Holmes (October 1970)
Poland 23 x 33 in (58 x 84 cm)

Right:
The Private Life of Sherlock Holmes (October 1970)
US 11 x 14 in (28 x 36 cm)

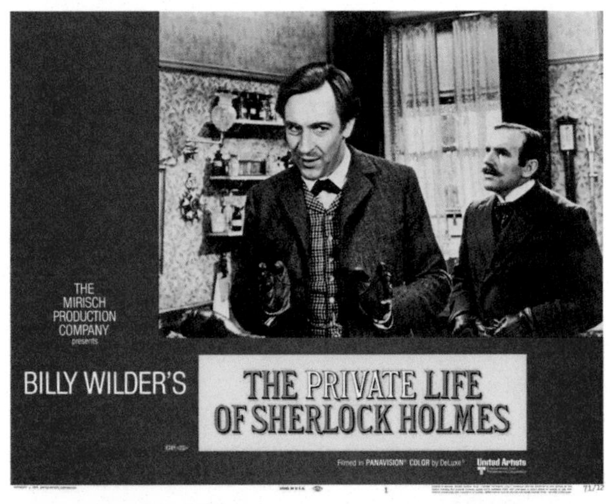
THE MIRISCH PRODUCTION COMPANY presents
BILLY WILDER'S
THE PRIVATE LIFE OF SHERLOCK HOLMES
Filmed in PANAVISION® COLOR by DeLuxe®
United Artists

THE MIRISCH PRODUCTION COMPANY presents
BILLY WILDER'S
THE PRIVATE LIFE OF SHERLOCK HOLMES
Filmed in PANAVISION® COLOR by DeLuxe®
United Artists

THE MIRISCH PRODUCTION COMPANY presents
BILLY WILDER'S
THE PRIVATE LIFE OF SHERLOCK HOLMES
Filmed in PANAVISION® COLOR by DeLuxe®
United Artists

THE MIRISCH PRODUCTION COMPANY presents
BILLY WILDER'S
THE PRIVATE LIFE OF SHERLOCK HOLMES
Filmed in PANAVISION® COLOR by DeLuxe®
United Artists

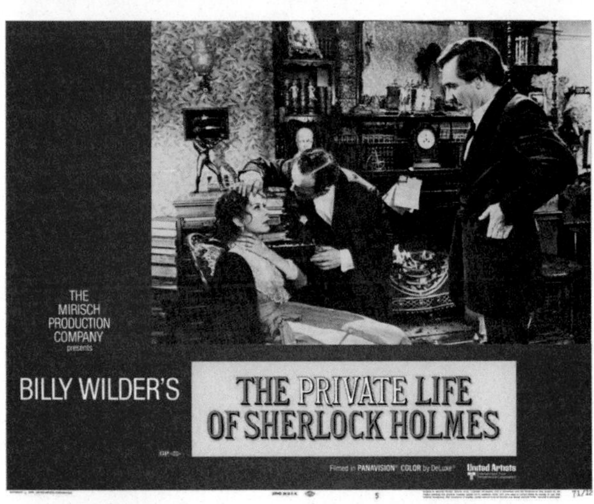
THE MIRISCH PRODUCTION COMPANY presents
BILLY WILDER'S
THE PRIVATE LIFE OF SHERLOCK HOLMES
Filmed in PANAVISION® COLOR by DeLuxe®
United Artists

THE MIRISCH PRODUCTION COMPANY presents
BILLY WILDER'S
THE PRIVATE LIFE OF SHERLOCK HOLMES
Filmed in PANAVISION® COLOR by DeLuxe®
United Artists

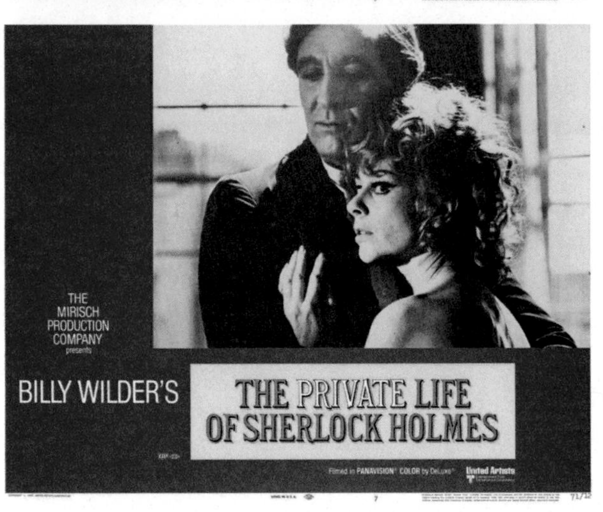
THE MIRISCH PRODUCTION COMPANY presents
BILLY WILDER'S
THE PRIVATE LIFE OF SHERLOCK HOLMES
Filmed in PANAVISION® COLOR by DeLuxe®
United Artists

THE MIRISCH PRODUCTION COMPANY presents
BILLY WILDER'S
THE PRIVATE LIFE OF SHERLOCK HOLMES
Filmed in PANAVISION® COLOR by DeLuxe®
United Artists

Sherlock Holmes' Smarter Brother (December 1975)
US 27 x 41 in (69 x 104 cm)

The Seven-Percent-Solution (October 1976)
US 27 x 41 in (69 x 104 cm)

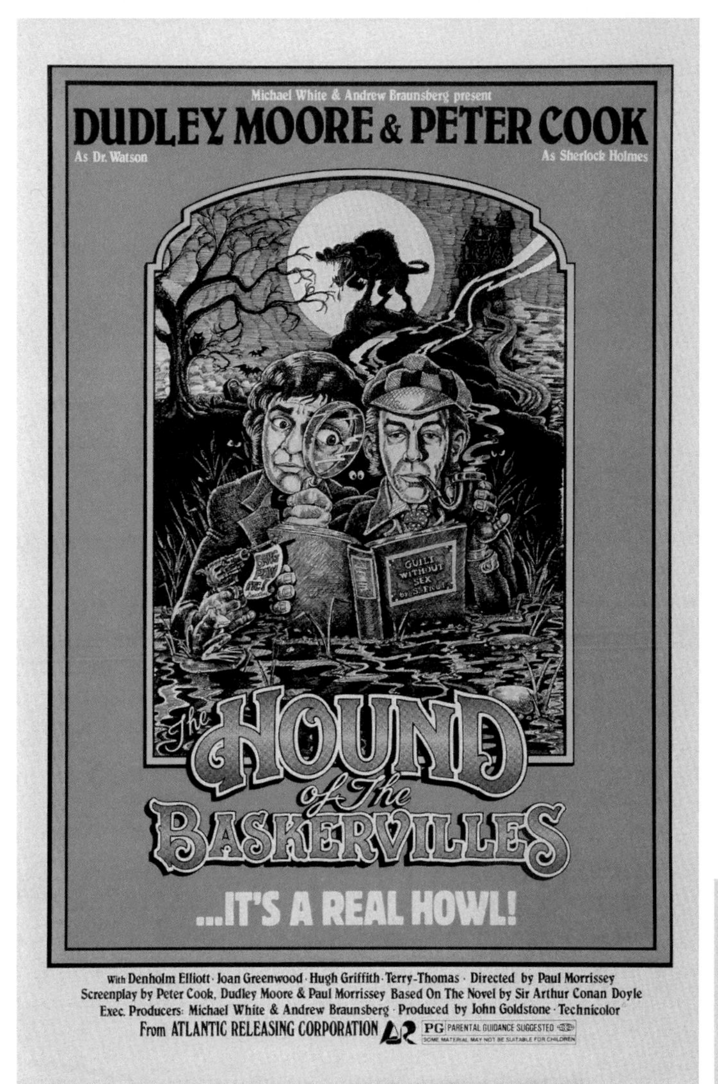

The Hound of the Baskervilles (October 1978 - UK)
US 27 x 41 in (69 x 104 cm)

Murder By Decree (February 1979)
US 27 x 41 in (69 x 104 cm)

Sherlock Holmes and the Masks of Death (December 1984)
Czechoslovakian 11 x 16 in (28 x 41 cm)

Young Sherlock Holmes (December 1985)
AKA: “Pyramid of Fear”
Czechoslovakian 11 x 16 in (28 x 41 cm)

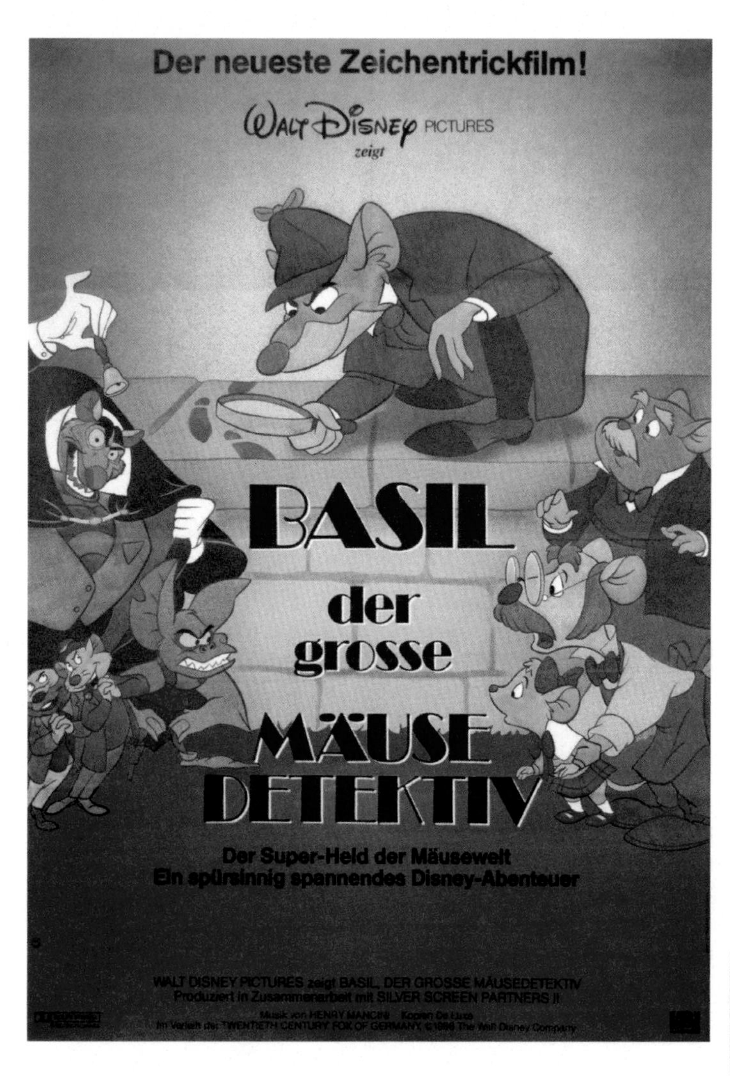

The Great Mouse Detective (July 1986)
Germany 23 x 33 in (58 x 84 cm)

Without A Clue (October 1988)
Poland 26 x 38 in (66 x 97 cm)

The Long Awaited Return

After a twenty-year absence, Sherlock returned in a big way with *Sherlock Holmes* (2009), the most action-packed film in the franchise's history. Academy Award-nominated actors Robert Downey Jr. and Jude Law won Sherlock Holmes a new generation of fans.

Sherlock Holmes (December 2009)
US 27 x 40 in (69 x 102 cm)

The story, set in 1890's London, starts with Sherlock (Robert Downey Jr.) rushing to save a young woman from a ritualistic sacrificial death at the hands of Lord Blackwood (Mark Strong). Three months later, we find a tormented Holmes at Baker St. suffering from an apparent hangover and depression over the impending departure of his partner Dr. John Watson (Jude Law), who is destined to wed his sweetheart, Mary Morstan (Kelly Reilly), and ultimately dissolve their partnership.

Lord Blackwood communicates his final request to prison authorities, requesting to speak with Holmes. Blackwood tells Holmes that his reign of terror is not over, and that three more souls are yet to be lost. He opines that Holmes himself will be responsible for these deaths. A short time later, the sentence is carried out, Blackwood is hanged, and pronounced dead by Dr. Watson.

Inspector Lestrade (Eddie Marsan) requests Holmes' presence to discuss the apparent resurrection of the recently departed Blackwood. Later, at the cemetery a group of less than eager constables exhume the coffin, finding it occupied by Luke Reordan (Oran Gurel), rather than Blackwood.

With the help of a watch, liberated from Reordan's pocket, Holmes is directed to the Maddison & Haig Pawn Shop, where he is able to ascertain Reordan's home address. The search of the laboratory like residence reveals that Reordan had been working with Blackwood...but to what end? As Holmes and Watson continue to investigate, they are joined by three miscreants sent to burn the building down, to destroy all evidence. A knock-down, drag out fight ensues, resulting in the loss of their evidence, and nearly their lives.

Holmes is next summoned to speak with the secret head of the Temple of The Four Orders, Sir Thomas Rotheram (James Fox), where the organization tries to enlist his assistance in finding the not so dead Lord Blackwood. Holmes surmises that Sir Thomas is actually the father of Blackwood and warns him that he may not be long for this earth now that his son had returned from the grave. Holmes tells the Order that he will find Blackwood, but only on his terms. Unfortunately for Sir Thomas, Holmes was right, and he did not make it through the night.

In a strange, but planned turn of events, Lord Blackwood is elevated to head of the Temple of the Four Orders, and using his dark magic causes his only decenter to burst into flames and die, quickly bringing to remaining members of the Order into acceptance of their new leader.

Circling back to an earlier assailant, Holmes determines that visiting a factory on the docks may help lead them to Blackwood. In a good news, bad new scenario, they find the right location, but also find that they have been set up by Blackwood, who has captured Holmes' love interest (Irene Adler), and they must act quickly to save her from certain death.

Holmes now finds himself a wanted fugitive, now that Blackwood, through Order member Lord Coward (Hans Matheson) has control of Scotland Yard. Holmes deduces Blackwood's plan is to kill members of the British Parliament to take control of the United Kingdom, and beyond. Sherlock allows himself to be captured by Lestrade so that he can learn the final pieces of Blackwood's plan from Lord Coward. With the covert help of Lestrade, Holmes is able to escape the Yard.

With the knowledge of Blackwood's plan, Holmes, Watson and Adler quickly make their way to Parliament, to foil Blackwood's evil endeavor. Working together, the three are able to stop Blackwood's "weapon of mass destruction". After a struggle, Bkackwood ultimately falls to his death. The story wraps with Adler telling Holmes that her employer was a fellow by the name of Professor Moriarty, who we later discover was ultimately trying to steal a key piece of technology from Blackwood's device.

SHERLOCK
HOLMES
SHERLOCK
HOLMES
SHERLOCK
HOLMES
SHERLOCK
HOLMES
SHERLOCK
HOLMES
SHERLOCK
HOLMES
SHERLOCK
HOLMES
SHERLOCK
HOLMES

Sherlock Holmes (December 2009)
US - Four Door Panel Compilation

Left:
Sherlock Holmes (December 2009)
US 11 x 14 in (28 x 36 cm)

Just two years later, Robert Downey Jr. returned to the streets of London, in *Sherlock Holmes: A Game of Shadows* (2011).

Sherlock (Robert Downey Jr.), disguised as what appears to be a homeless elderly Chinese man, is surveilling Irene Adler (Rachel McAdams) as she covertly receives a package handoff from a courier. Holmes approaches, slyly swaps her package for a loaf of bread and warns her that she is being followed. Despite the two making dinner plans, Sherlock's deduction turns out to be a less than elementary as Adler reveals that the men following her are actually escorting her, after which she retrieves her package, and leaves Holmes to deal with her accomplices.

Irene delivers the package, which is supposed to be payment for a business contact, Doctor Hoffmanstahl (Wolf Kahler), of her employer. Hoffmanstahl hands her an envelope, and she attempts to leave, however the doctor insists she stay while he confirms his payment. Holmes enters the room as the package is being opened, confiscates the envelope from Alder, and manages to halt the package from exploding. As Holmes exits the building he finds the doctor dead, a victim of a poisonous blow-dart.

Hours later, Irene is seated in a crowded restaurant, adjacent to a concealed Professor Moriarty (Jared Harris) who is anxious to retrieve the envelope which Hoffmanstahl had given Adler. When Irene explains that there was a complication, Moriarty quips that Sherlock has interfered with his plans too many times and vows to take care of him. He then informs Adler that he no longer requires her services, and she attempts to exit the establishment, but collapses on her way out, after apparently having been poisoned by Moriarty.

Sometime later, Dr. John Watson (Jude Law) visits 221b Baker St., to ensure Holmes will be ready to attend his wedding to his fiancée Mary Morstan (Kelly Reilly), the following morning. Watson finds a manic Holmes ranting about Moriarty, his involvement in Hoffmanstahl's death, and pondering his ultimate evil plan.

Holmes and Watson speed off in their horseless carriage in pursuit of an evening's celebration of John's last night of freedom. As they arrive at their destination, they are joined by Sherlock's brother Mycroft (Stephen Fry), who explains that he is concerned with the recent uptick in violence in Europe. To Watson's dismay, his stag party seems to lack any sort of planning, so he leaves Holmes to do some gambling on his own. Holmes ventures upstairs to visit Gypsy fortune teller, Madam Simza (Noomi Rapace), who it turns out was the intended recipient of the envelope that he took from Irene earlier. The envelope contained a letter from her brother Rene (Laurence Possa) saying that she would not see him again, as he "found his purpose in life". Simza is eager to dismiss Holmes without providing any details, however Sherlock informs her of would be assassins hiding in her room. An unavoidable brawl ensues, as Holmes tries to protect the Gypsy. The fight migrates downstairs, ultimately landing in the middle of Watson's game, and ultimately drawing him into a fight.

Back in their motorcar, Holmes chauffeurs the two, beaten and bruised, to John's wedding. Despite their disheveled appearance, the wedding goes off without a hitch...other than the one intended. As Holmes departs the festivities, Moriarty's lackey informs him that the professor would like to speak to him later that afternoon.

The professor inquires about the morning nuptials, to which Holmes informs him that with the ceremony completed, Watson is no longer associated with him. Moriarty, however, clarifies that collateral damage frequently occurs. He further eludes to the fact that Irene Adler was herself collateral damage. Holmes departs with Moriarty, declaring that he'll be sure to send his regards to the happy couple.

The newlyweds board a Brighton bound train, en route to their honeymoon, but are soon accosted by men, certainly sent by Moriarty. Holmes, in disguise as a less than handsome woman, assists the couple in fending off the assailants. Holmes ends up pushing Mary off the train, for a well-timed landing in a river, and a safe rendezvous with Mycroft. Holmes and Watson are successful at fending off the onslaught of assassins, and are shortly on their way to Paris, where Holmes expects to find some answers at the village of Madam Simza, the Gypsy fortune teller.

Sherlock and Watson find Simza and eventually determine that her brother Rene may be located at the hideout of an anarchist group, of which Simza and Rene had previously been members. Holmes is familiar with the group leader, Claude Ravache (Thierry Neuvic), a well-known bomb maker. Simza is certain that she can arrange a meeting with Ravache, in hopes of learning more about her brother.

Their meeting is cut short when Ravache pulls out a revolver and takes his own life, after saying that he has made a deal with the devil. Escaping out a secret door, the three head out in search of the intended bombing target. After some Moriarty misdirection, they arrive at the Hotel du Triomphe, just as the bomb explodes. While surveying the rubble, Holmes notices that a man by the name of Alfred Meinhard (Thorston Manderlay) had actually been shot and killed seconds before the blast. Meinhard's company produces weapons, and coincidently, recently had a portion of its stock purchased by an anonymous buyer.

His powers of deduction lead Holmes to the conclusion that Moriarty was, in fact, that anonymous buyer, and that he was soon to be on his way to the main factory in Heilbronn, Germany. Watson, Holmes and their Gypsy entourage are quickly on their way to Heilbronn. Holmes sends Watson on a mission to send a telegram to Mycroft, and then heads off to investigate the factory. While surveying the extensive weapons inventory, Holmes is captured and brought to Moriarty. Sherlock quickly realizes that the professor is determined to start a world war. Holmes is subsequently impaled with a large metal hook suspended from the ceiling, while Moriarty attempts to discover who the telegram was sent to.

Watson is able to rescue Holmes, and they, along with their Gypsy friends flee the scene, through a barrage of bullets and mortars from the factory base. Narrowly escaping, the group hops on a train, ultimately making their way to Switzerland, where they believe Moriarty will strike next, at the upcoming peace summit.

Moriarty is a guest at the opening ball of the summit, which Holmes surveils to try to discern his plan. Realizing that he plans to use Rene to assassinate attending officials, Holmes leaves Watson and Simza to circumvent the plot. In the meantime, Holmes meets Moriarty on the balcony, for a quick game of chess. As the two are locked in board game combat, Holmes reveals that he has foiled Moriarty's plan, and subsequently robbed him of his considerable wealth. Enraged, Moriarty engages Holmes who realizes that he cannot overpower Moriarty, so he pulls him over the railing and the two plummet into the cold, wet abyss below. Despite this turn of events, in this case nothing is elementary.

Sherlock Holmes: A Game of Shadows (December 2011)
Japan 7 x 10 in (18 x 25 cm)

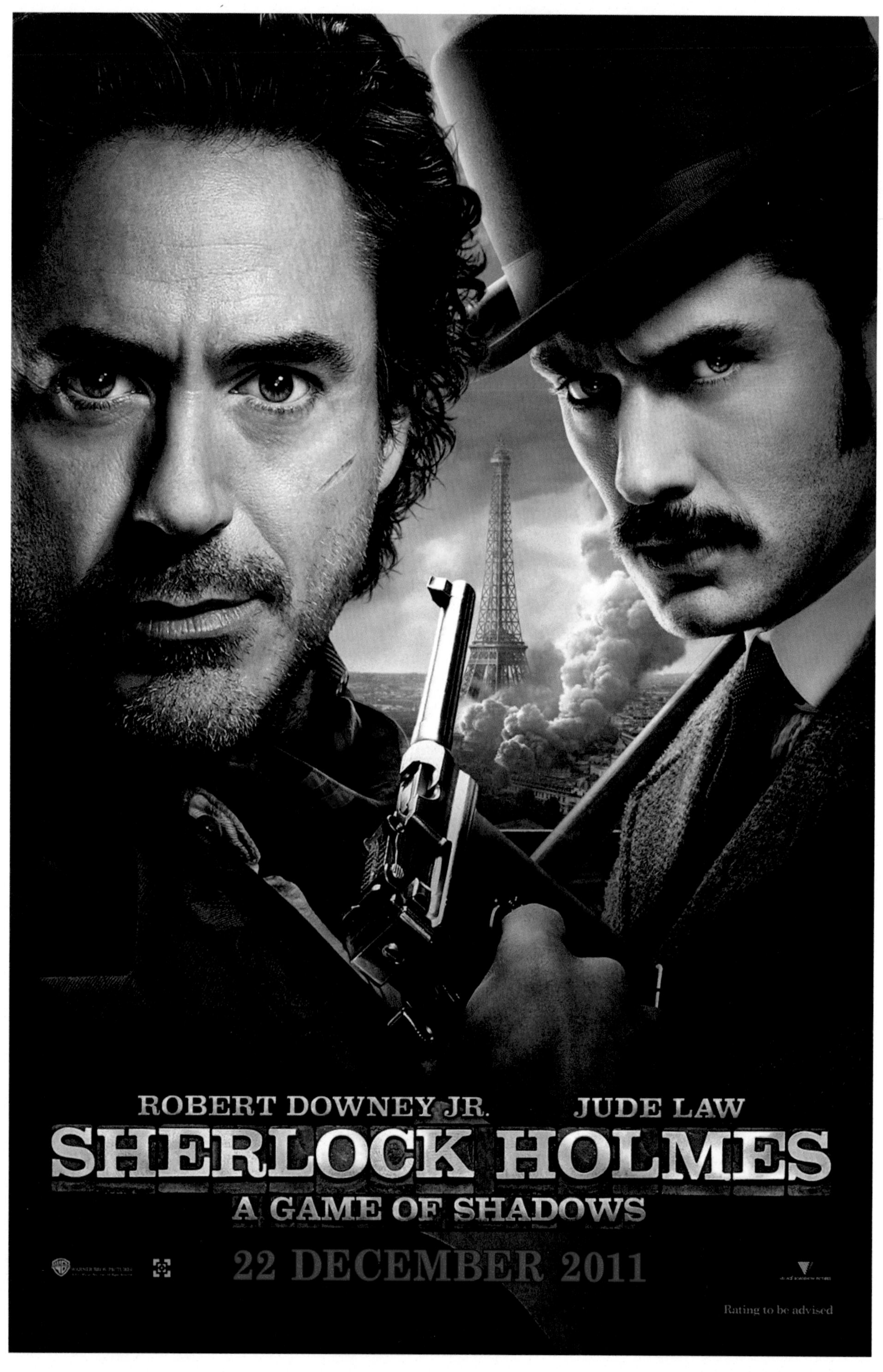

Sherlock Holmes: A Game of Shadows (December 2011)
US 27 x 40 in (69 x 102 cm)

CPSIA information can be obtained
at www.ICGtesting.com
Printed in the USA
LVIC06n1206301117
557585LV00004B/14